The
Calligraphy
Handbook

The Calligraphy Handbook

Simple techniques and step-by-step projects

Emma Callery

CHARTWELL
BOOKS

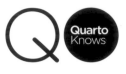

Brimming with creative inspiration, how-to projects, and useful information to enrich your everyday life, Quarto Knows is a favorite destination for those pursuing their interests and passions. Visit our site and dig deeper with our books into your area of interest: Quarto Creates, Quarto Cooks, Quarto Homes, Quarto Lives, Quarto Drives, Quarto Explores, Quarto Gifts, or Quarto Kids.

Inspiring | Educating | Creating | Entertaining

Chartwell Books

© 2018 Quarto Publishing PLC

This edition published in 2018
by Chartwell Books,
an imprint of The Quarto Group
142 West 36th Street, 4th Floor
New York, NY 10018 USA
T (212) 779-4972 F (212) 779-6058
www.QuartoKnows.com

10 9 8 7 6 5 4 3 2 1

Chartwell Books titles are also available at discount for retail, wholesale, promotional, and bulk purchase. For details, contact the Special Sales Manager by email at specialsales@quarto.com or by mail at The Quarto Group, Attn: Special Sales Manager, 401 Second Avenue North, Suite 310, Minneapolis, MN 55401, USA.

ISBN: 978-0-7858-3668-1
BP. CABO

Printed in China

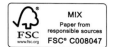

Revised Edition Designer: Lindsey Johns
Art Director: Simon Thompson
Photography: Paul Forrester
Editors: Anne Johnson, Jo Silman
Senior Editor: Marian Broderick
Publisher: Gaynor Sermon

The material in this publication previously appeared in *The Calligraphy Source Book, An Introduction to Calligraphy, The Encyclopedia of Calligraphy Techniques, The Art and Craft of Calligraphy,* and *The Complete Calligrapher.*

Acknowledgments

Step-by-step sequences demonstrated by Diane Hardy Wilson, Annie Moring, and George Evans.

The right of Diane Hardy Wilson to be identified as the author of *The Encyclopedia of Calligraphy Techniques* from which the work on pages 10, 11, 27, 28, 30, 31, 33, 35, 37, 65, 67, 68, 69. 71, 72, 73, 77, 78, 79, 81, 82, 83, 84, 85, 87, 88, 89, 91, 94, 95, 97, 98, 99, 100, 101, 102, 103, 107, 108, 109, 121, 123, 125, 129, 131, 137, 138, 139, 140, 142, 156, 157, 159, 159 and 174 has been taken, has been asserted by her in accordance with the Copyright, Designs and Patents Act 1988.

15 (far right) Wisiel/ Shutterstock;
18 Steve Gorton/ Getty Images; 34 Paul Shaw;
85 Ieuan Rees; 113, 115, 132-134, 144-145, 148-151, 154-155 Miriam Stribley; 117 Peter Thompson;
118-119 Arthur Baker; 126-127 Dorothy Mahoney;
135 Evert van Dijk; 146-147, 183 based on Hans Meyer, Graphis; 152-153, 165-167, 170-171, 173, 177-179, 182, 185, 187 Dover Publications; 164, 169 V&A Museum.

Every effort has been made to obtain copyright clearance, and we apologize for any omissions.

MIX
Paper from responsible sources
FSC® C008047

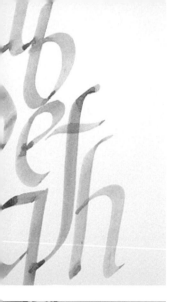

CONTENTS

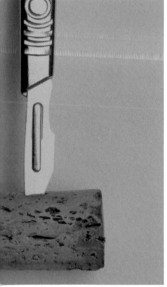

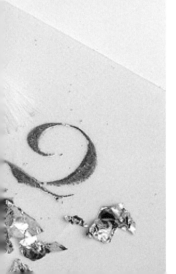

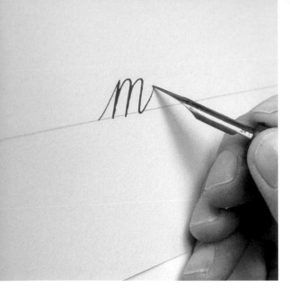
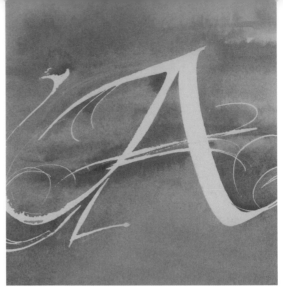

INTRODUCTION

The techniques, tools, materials, and some of the letterforms are much the same now as they were in the medieval period in Europe. However, this doesn't mean that calligraphy has no part to play in the modern world.

This book is concerned both with the working methods of practicing calligraphers and with what they want their calligraphy to "perform." In the USA and Europe, readers expect to see letters running from left to right and from top to bottom in straight lines of varying length. However, wherever he or she lives, the calligrapher has wonderful opportunities to break free from the traditional mold, and make letters perform visually as well as intellectually.

The modern student of calligraphy turns to historical models for an understanding of letterforms, as used by earlier professionals. Before the invention of printing, calligraphy was vitally important as one of the few means

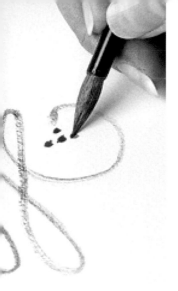
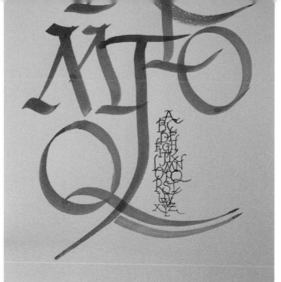
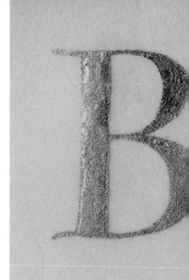

The craft of calligraphy—a Greek word meaning "beautiful writing"—has roots that stretch back into the mists of time.

of storing and transmitting the written word. For centuries scribes produced books by hand and we still have much to learn from their methods.

Print is primarily for reading, not for seeing. The vast amounts of written material to which we are exposed every day make us switch off our sensitivity to lettering. Information bombards us—from sensation-filled newspapers, to information on packaged products, to road signs, store signs, and street names. The act of reading has become an everyday skill that most of us take for granted.

Calligraphy helps us to see what we are reading by making the words themselves beautiful. Though much of its impact relies upon producing a rhythmic texture in the writing, the beauty is not necessarily peaceful. Tensions can also be used to disturb us. Seen in this light, calligraphy is a powerful tool for communicating the written word in the modern world.

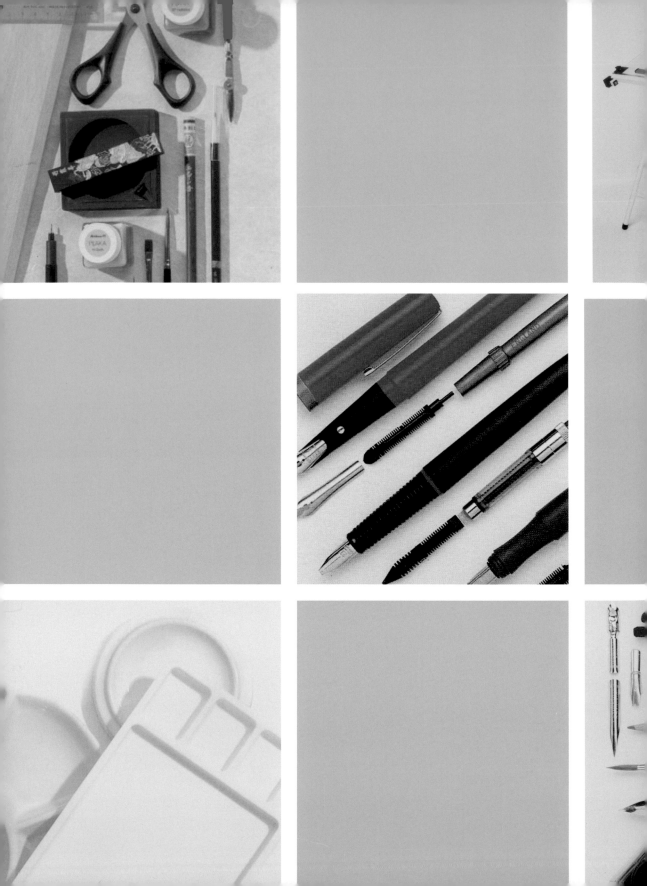

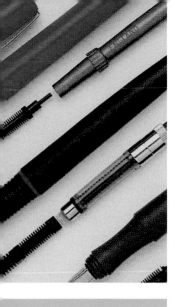

TOOLS AND EQUIPMENT

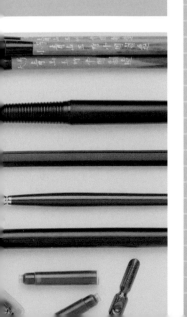

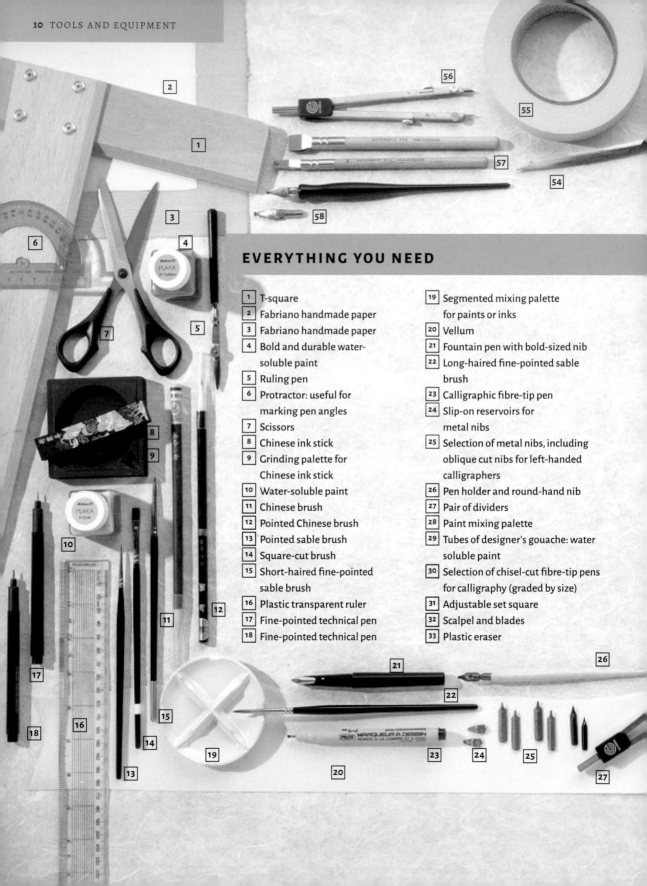

EVERYTHING YOU NEED

1 T-square
2 Fabriano handmade paper
3 Fabriano handmade paper
4 Bold and durable water-soluble paint
5 Ruling pen
6 Protractor: useful for marking pen angles
7 Scissors
8 Chinese ink stick
9 Grinding palette for Chinese ink stick
10 Water-soluble paint
11 Chinese brush
12 Pointed Chinese brush
13 Pointed sable brush
14 Square-cut brush
15 Short-haired fine-pointed sable brush
16 Plastic transparent ruler
17 Fine-pointed technical pen
18 Fine-pointed technical pen

19 Segmented mixing palette for paints or inks
20 Vellum
21 Fountain pen with bold-sized nib
22 Long-haired fine-pointed sable brush
23 Calligraphic fibre-tip pen
24 Slip-on reservoirs for metal nibs
25 Selection of metal nibs, including oblique cut nibs for left-handed calligraphers
26 Pen holder and round-hand nib
27 Pair of dividers
28 Paint mixing palette
29 Tubes of designer's gouache: water soluble paint
30 Selection of chisel-cut fibre-tip pens for calligraphy (graded by size)
31 Adjustable set square
32 Scalpel and blades
33 Plastic eraser

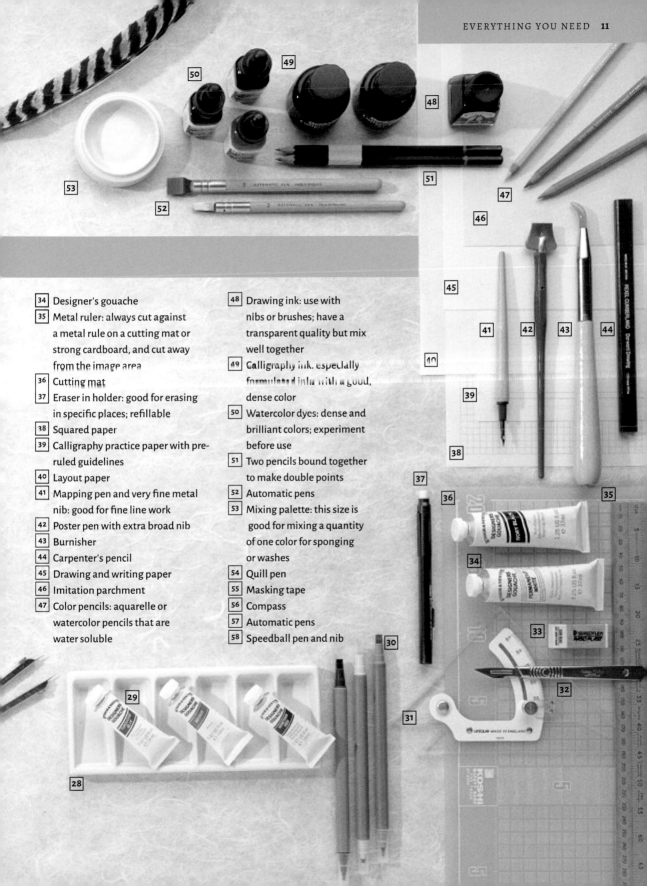

34 Designer's gouache

35 Metal ruler: always cut against
a metal rule on a cutting mat or
strong cardboard, and cut away
from the image area

36 Cutting mat

37 Eraser in holder: good for erasing
in specific places; refillable

38 Squared paper

39 Calligraphy practice paper with pre-
ruled guidelines

40 Layout paper

41 Mapping pen and very fine metal
nib: good for fine line work

42 Poster pen with extra broad nib

43 Burnisher

44 Carpenter's pencil

45 Drawing and writing paper

46 Imitation parchment

47 Color pencils: aquarelle or
watercolor pencils that are
water soluble

48 Drawing ink: use with
nibs or brushes; have a
transparent quality but mix
well together

49 Calligraphy ink: especially
formulated inks with a good,
dense color

50 Watercolor dyes: dense and
brilliant colors; experiment
before use

51 Two pencils bound together
to make double points

52 Automatic pens

53 Mixing palette: this size is
good for mixing a quantity
of one color for sponging
or washes

54 Quill pen

55 Masking tape

56 Compass

57 Automatic pens

58 Speedball pen and nib

Writing Tools

The craft of calligraphy does not require a large capital outlay, though there are a few essentials that you cannot do without. The main requirements are simple enough—pen, ink, and paper—and the most important ingredient of all, a willingness to learn. But don't rush out and buy just any old pen. Take your time, read these pages carefully, and then make your decision.

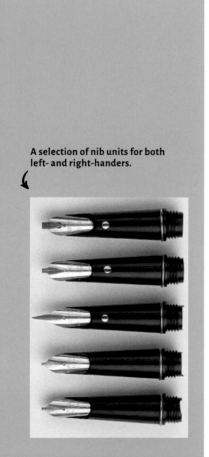

A selection of nib units for both left- and right-handers.

There are two main types of steel-nibbed pen: the pen nib with reservoir and pen holder, which requires constant filling; and the fountain-type pen, which has a built-in reservoir. The latter is a better choice for the beginner. It relieves you of the tedious task of constantly refilling the reservoir, using a paintbrush or pipette that then requires washing out, before continuing to letter. Full concentration is needed and so any distraction or encumbrance should be avoided.

Whichever type of pen you choose, always inform the supplier whether the user will be right- or left-handed. There are special nibs for left-handed people, where the end of the nib slopes top right to bottom left when viewed from the top. Whichever pen collection is chosen, there will be a variety of nib sizes available, although the size of, say, an Italic fine may vary between different manufacturers, whether it is intended to be used for a fountain pen or a nib holder.

FOUNTAIN PENS

There are various calligraphic pens on the market. Some are purchased as an integral unit (that is, a complete pen); others are bought as a set and include a barrel, reservoir, and a set of interchangeable nib units. Avoid the cartridge refill as it limits the color of ink that can be used. It is better to buy a pen that has a squeeze-fill reservoir so that color can be changed quite easily.

Don't be afraid to ask your local art store to show you their entire range. The choice of pens available is constantly increasing and you must ensure that you choose the one that is the most comfortable for you. The larger suppliers often have demonstration pens that can be tested before your final decision to make a purchase.

NIBS

Once you have gained confidence and experience with a pen, a pen holder and range of nibs will be the next addition to your equipment. The range available is vast, including round-hand, script, poster, scroll, and special-effect nibs. These items are sold separately or can often be bought on a display card, which contains a pen holder, reservoir, and set of nibs. If you purchase this type of pen, you will need to remove the film of lacquer coating the nibs in order to avoid deterioration. This can be done either by passing the nib through a flame or by gently scraping the surface.

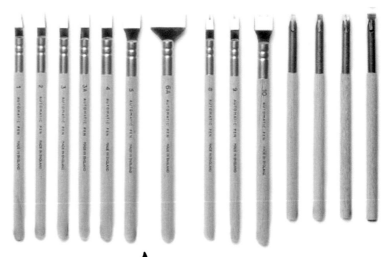

A selection of writing tools.

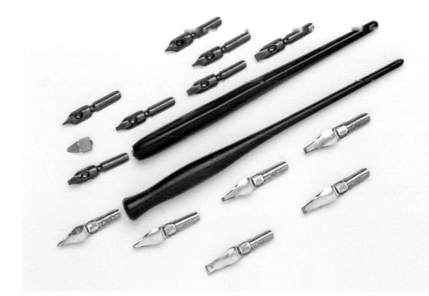

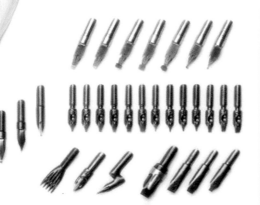

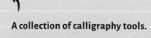

Pen nibs and holders with an ink reservoir, and nibs with integral reservoirs.

A collection of calligraphy tools.

Ink and Paper

There are many inks available, and the choice is made difficult by this fact. The main property an ink should have is that it should flow easily and not clog the pen. Non-waterproof ink flows marginally better than waterproof inks and watercolors. The medium should not spread on the writing surface. Unwanted feathering can be attributed either to the paper or to the ink, and you should experiment with both in order to confirm compatibility.

Density of color is important in finished work, and there are inks available that are specifically stated as being calligraphic inks. These are suitable for use in fountain-type pens. There are also inks that are referred to as "artist color," some of which are waterproof; many need a cleaning fluid to clean or flush the pen through after use.

(Check with the stockist that such a cleaning agent will have no harmful effects.) The range of colors is wide, and most of these types of ink are mixable, giving an even wider range.

Calligraphers often use watercolor paint for embellishment. This is satisfactory for a pen and holder but not for a fountain pen. Rather than watercolor, pens can be

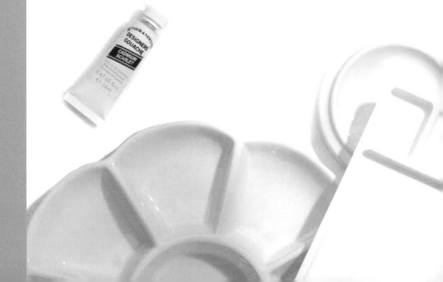

filled with an artist's retouching dye, which is translucent and water soluble; as a result, the color is very pure. Inks and watercolors vary in light fastness, so check the label for the product's degree of permanence.

Some bottles have a pipette incorporated in the cap. This is useful for charging the reservoirs in pen holders, and saves loading with a brush.

PAPER

For the beginner, a designer's layout pad is ideal for roughing out ideas and preliminary penwork. Pads come in various sizes, finishes, and weights. Initially, choose a paper that is not too opaque and make sure that, when the paper is placed over the sample alphabets in the book, you can still see the letterforms through it.

There are also typo pads available that are specifically made for designers' layouts. This type of pad is ideal, because it is used for tracing letters in studios when laying out work.

Different papers for finished work, available in pads or single sheets.

It has a milky white appearance and is not as transparent as tracing paper.

A good-quality writing or drawing paper is best for finished work. Writing papers are produced in many shades and finishes, although they can be a little restrictive as a result of the sizes available. There are also many drawing papers that can be put to good use. It is as well to experiment with different types of paper, avoiding those with a heavy coating, as they obstruct the passage of the nib and flow of ink. For outdoor work, such as posters, it is advisable to use a special paper that weathers well, but do not forget to use a waterproof ink.

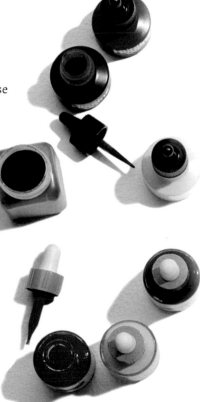

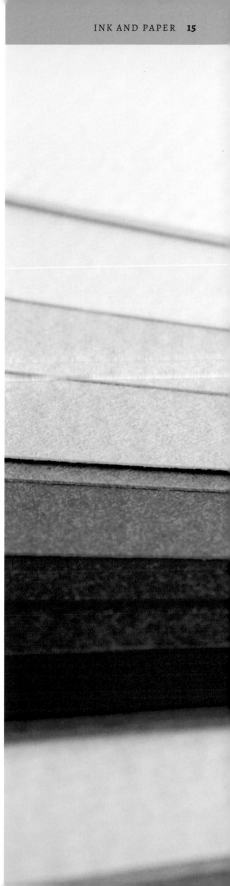

Additional Tools

Other things you will need are listed below. As well as these, you will also need masking tape and a few large sheets of cartridge paper to cover the new board and to guard any work. An absorbent cloth, or kitchen paper, will also be necessary to wipe the fountain pen clean after filling, and to wipe the nib when the ink shows signs of building up or clogging.

When the scalpel is not in use, use a cork to prevent accidents and avoid blunting the blade.

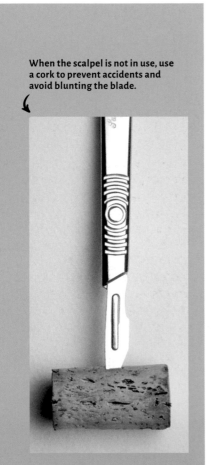

Some double-sided tape and a substantial weight of card will also be required, as will some additional lighting if the working area lacks either sufficient daylight or good artificial light. Lighting is discussed in more detail in the next chapter.

RULER

Choose a 18in (450mm) ruler, preferably with both imperial and metric calibrations. Transparent rulers with grid lines running parallel to their edges can be useful for horizontal alignment in rough layouts, where multiple lines need ruling. A ruler with a good beveled edge is more accurate for transferring measurements and is useful when reversed for ruling ink lines as the beveled edge prevents ink seeping under the ruler.

SET SQUARE

A 45° set square is required. Some have millimeter calibrations on the right-angled edges, and these are useful when laying out rectangular shapes. The square should be at least 10in (250mm) on the two shorter edges. A similar 30°/60° set square is also needed.

PENCILS

Use a hard pencil for marking preliminary guidelines, which need to be fine. The leads are not too soft, so you won't have to spend a lot of time keeping the point sharp. You will also need a soft pencil for rough layout work, in order to give a good image without undue pressure. A soft carpenter's pencil is good for initial test layouts and can be sharpened to a chisel edge to emulate the size of a calligraphic nib. Propelling,

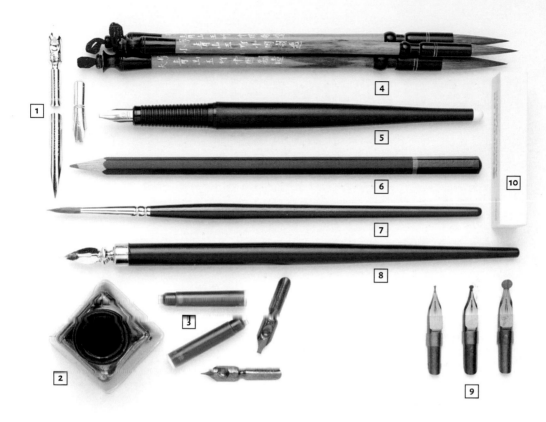

or clutch, pencils have become very popular in recent years. A $\frac{1}{50}$ in (0.5mm) lead size is preferable, as the smaller leads tend to snap.

ERASER

There are many erasers on the market. Choose a plastic one for paper and film.

CUTTING TOOL

A surgical scalpel has an exceptionally keen edge and is useful. Replacement blades are often sold in units of five per packet.

Be careful when changing the blade, as it is extremely sharp and should be treated with great respect. Always remove the blade by lifting it first from its retaining lug and then, using your thumb, push the blade away from the body. Keep the fingers well away from contact with the cutting edge.

When fitting a new blade, slide it onto the retaining lug, grip the blade on the blunt top edge, and push it home. When the scalpel is not in use, it is a good idea to cover the blade with an old wine cork, which will keep your fingers away from it. This prevents accidents as well as avoiding blunting the blade.

EQUIPMENT

1 gold-plated nibs
2 ink
3 ink cartridges
4 Chinese brushes
5 cartridge pen
6 pencil
7 paint brush
8 dip pen
9 special nibs
10 eraser

Drawing Boards

You will need a drawing board on which to work. This does not need to be an expensive purchase. In calligraphy, work is done with the drawing board at an angle. Position yourself in front of the work so that you can see it clearly without stretching. The angle of the board should ideally be at about 45°. However, providing that you are in a good viewing position, it may be as low as 30°.

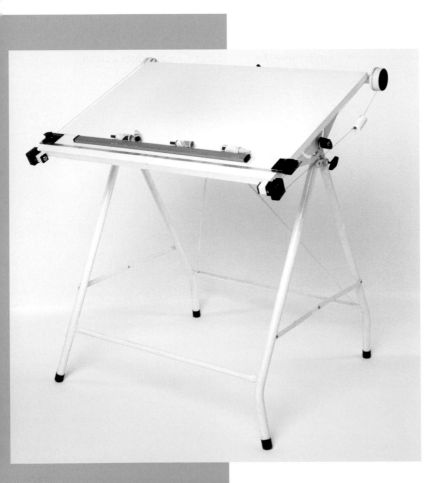

Never work on a flat surface as this necessitates bending over the board and using the pen in an upright position, whereas the pen will be at a shallower angle on a sloping board, helping to regulate the flow of ink.

A drawing board can be purchased, with or without adjustable angles, from most art stores. Alternatively, laminate shelving board is available at most timber merchants and is quite adequate. A suitable board size is 18 x 24in (450 x 600mm). Apply iron-on laminate edges to give a clean finish.

The board can be supported on your lap and leaned against a table or desk, making an angle of about 45° with the desk top.

A professional drawing board with parallel motion.

HOME-MADE DRAWING BOARD

A professional-looking board that adjusts to three angles can be made quite readily.

INSTRUCTIONS

Cut two laminate boards to the dimensions above, one for the base and the other for the top. Cut a further piece in the same material for the board support and use some softwood for support battens, table stop, and board-base spacer. All these items measure the same width as the drawing board. In addition, six butt hinges and some chipboard screws will be required.

Screw a board spacer to one edge of the base, together with a table stop on the opposite side to prevent the board from sliding when in use.

Screw the support battens to the base in the positions shown, to give three angles from approximately 30° to 45°.

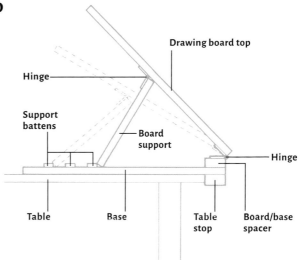

Attach the board support to the drawing board top with three of the hinges—one in the center and one a little distance in from each end. In order to achieve the desired angles it is essential to position the support correctly.

Fix the remaining three hinges to the underside of the drawing board at the base, with the other side to the board-base spacer. Give all edges a clean finish with iron-on laminate.

A home-made drawing board with three adjustable angles.

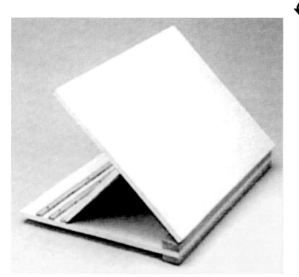

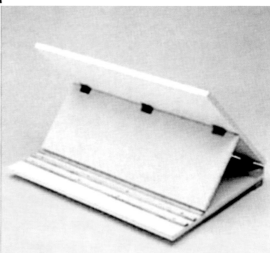

A card support for right-handed students.

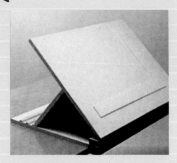

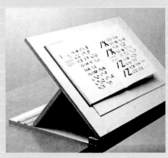

A card support for left-handed students.

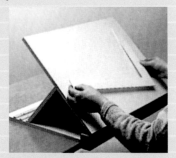

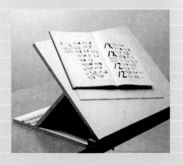

SETTING UP TO TRACE

First of all, the drawing board has to be set up so that this book can be used as a tracing reference. If you are right-handed, take a strip of heavy mounting card and position it with tape on the writing surface. This is where you will rest the book when the letterforms are traced.

Left- and right-handers

The card is positioned differently for left-handed students, because it is difficult for them to letter horizontally, as the writing hand tends to obscure their lettering. Establishing the correct angle of writing can involve an uncomfortable pen hold, even when using a left-handed nib. The problem will be lessened if you tilt the paper. So, if you are left-handed, try positioning the work with its right-hand side dropped down 15° from the horizontal, with the extra piece at right angles to prevent the book sliding to the right.

You can then try lettering a few characters. If you find the position uncomfortable, you may need to adjust the angle and you may even need to change it several times.

If you find that, by merely turning the paper through various degrees, you are still unable to achieve the desired angle of lettering, try grinding down the nib to form an even steeper angle. This can be done on a fine-grade India stone or fine-grade production paper (the type used by automobile sprayers to prepare paintwork).

But to save undue expense, experiment first with a nib that is used with a pen holder before attempting to convert a fountain-pen nib. In this way, at least, if the result is not satisfactory, a relatively costly nib will not have been ruined. Make sure, too, that, when you grind down the edge, a burr is not left on one side, nor the edge left so sharp as to cut into the surface of the paper to be lettered. Finally, ensure that the edge of the nib is square, not rounded.

YOUR POSITION WHEN LETTERING

It is important to be comfortable when seated, with the feet flat on the floor, the back straight, and the drawing board positioned so that the arms can move freely.

The height of the seat or chair used is important, and consideration should be given to the height of the table or desk on which the drawing board sits. If the board is too low, the calligrapher will inevitably acquire backache through bending over it; if too high, the neck and arms will suffer through constant stretching. The ideal height will differ for each and every one of you, and adjustments to seating and height of drawing board may be necessary.

SETTING UP FOR GENERAL WORK

Remove the pieces of card that you have used to keep the book in position. Now take two sheets of paper and cut them to a size that is 3in (75mm) less than the height and width of the surface area of the drawing board. If the board has been constructed from the illustration in this book (see page 19), this will be 15 x 21in (375 x 525mm).

Place the sheets of paper on the surface of the board with an equal border all around of about 1½in (40mm). Using masking tape, stick both sheets together to the board (see below). This will be easier if it is done with the board flat. Attach one of the long edges of the sheets first, then pull the sheets taut and stick down the opposite side. Tape the two exposed ends.

For the pad, cut a further, slightly larger sheet of paper, which will give a border of 1in (25mm) on the drawing board, and stick this with tape on all four edges so that no edge is left exposed and the sheet is taut. This will now provide an ideal writing surface. The pen does not perform as well on a hard, solid surface as when the backing sheets give a little spring for the nib. Once the first alphabet has been lettered, you should have a good idea of the point on the board where you feel most comfortable. This position will differ according to the individual and is known as the writing level.

LIGHTING

Correct lighting is as important for the eyes as posture is for the limbs. Tired eyes and limbs are not conducive to clean, crisp calligraphy. Ideally, you should work in daylight. If you are right-handed, the light source should come from your left; if left-handed, from your right. This should ensure that you are not working in the shadow cast by your writing hand. Lighting therefore plays a key role in the layout of the working area. Strong direct light, such as sunlight, should be avoided, as glare from the surface on which you are working, which is often white, will make lettering difficult.

GUARD SHEETS

To prevent grease being deposited from your hand onto the writing sheet, make a guard sheet from another sheet of paper. This must be positioned on the pad with tape, at a level that allows you to work on the writing line. To retain the writing sheet as it is moved toward the top of the board at the end of each line of lettering, you may use a strip of fabric tape or card at the top of the board. This is an optional extra.

Always put aside a spare piece of the writing material being used to start the pen off and to practice the strokes.

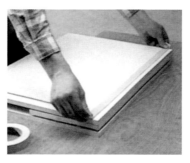

1 Apply masking tape to the top of the drawing board.

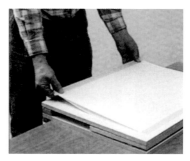

2 Apply masking tape to the bottom and pull cover taut.

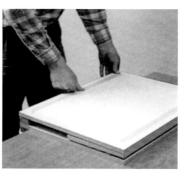

3 Stick both pages firmly down to the board.

Maintaining Your Pens

For some people, pens are not the easiest of tools to work with: they blot, dry up in the midst of a stroke, or even refuse to write at all. However, many of the complaints levelled at pens are due to poor maintenance. Just as with any other implement, they need a certain amount of care and attention if they are to perform properly.

Three kinds of fountain-type pens. The top two have interchangeable nib units. The third art pen is a complete unit, which is available in a number of sizes. The ink holders, or reservoirs, are of either the squeeze or piston type.

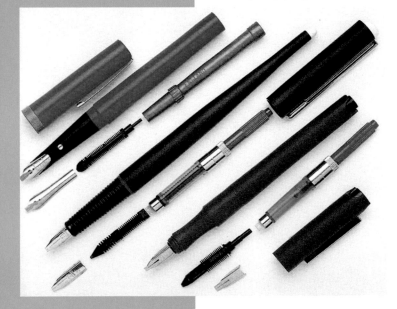

Always empty a fountain-type pen of ink after use, unless it is to be re-used within a short space of time. Ink quickly dries both on the nib and in the ink-feed section, soon rendering the pen completely useless. Time and effort can be saved by emptying the reservoir into the ink bottle and flushing the pen with lukewarm water containing a drop of dishwashing liquid. This simple measure is ideal for water-based inks and should keep the pen in good condition at all times.

PROBLEM-SOLVING

If the ink stops in the middle of a stroke, remove the barrel and squeeze or turn the reservoir, depending on the type of pen, until the ink reaches the nib. Make sure you have a paper towel on hand to prevent a disaster.

A pen that is drying or missing during writing may have insufficient ink, or the split in the nib may have become widened by pressure. Try filling the pen or reducing the split in the nib by squeezing both sides together.

Also check that the nib and ink duct are free from particles picked up from the paper surface. Ink will not take to a greasy surface.

STRIPPING DOWN

Occasionally, it may be necessary to strip down the whole nib unit and to clean it with soapy water and an old toothbrush or nail brush. This may seem excessive, but when changing color from, say, black to red, merely flushing the pen is insufficient to remove all the black ink, and the red or lighter color will be tainted if the pen is not completely clean. Similarly, if a pen has been left with ink inside for a period of time, without use, it will require stripping down in the same manner. A pipe cleaner is ideal for removing ink from inside the squeeze type reservoirs, but make sure that its wire center does not puncture the plastic.

There are now many different waterproof inks available for use in fountain pens, in a vast range of colors. These are difficult to remove with a water-based solution once the pen is left for even a short time because waterproof ink will dry up.

There is a cleaner available that is primarily used by airbrush artists for removing the color from the airbrush. This solution is ideal for a thorough strip-down operation. The fluid does not have any harmful effect on the pen and removes even the hardened ink, but it is always best to ask the supplier if it is safe to use on plastics.

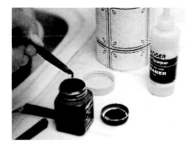

1 Empty the ink from the pen.

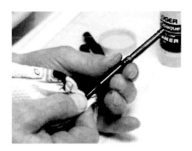

2 Remove the nib and ink feeder from its housing.

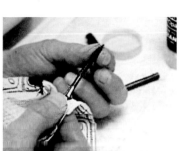

3 Separate the nib from the ink feeder.

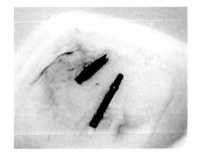

4 Wash out the housing and ink holder/reservoir, in water.

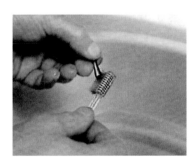

5 Use cleaning fluid and a toothbrush to clean the parts.

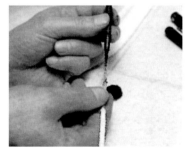

6 Use a pipe cleaner and fluid to clean inside the ink holder.

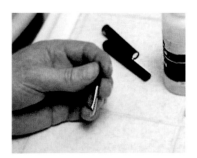

7 Align the nib and ink feeder.

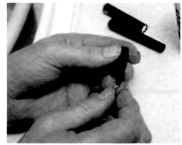

8 Reassemble the pen and fill with ink.

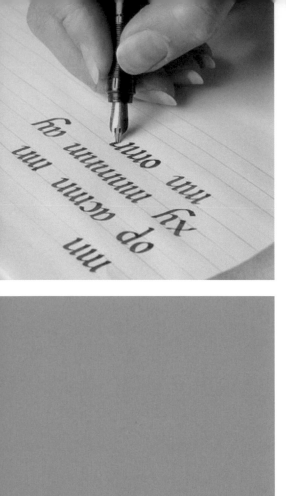
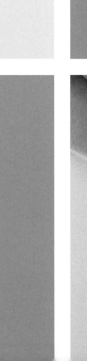
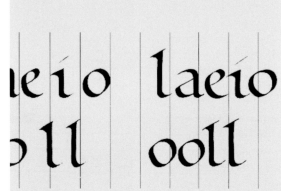
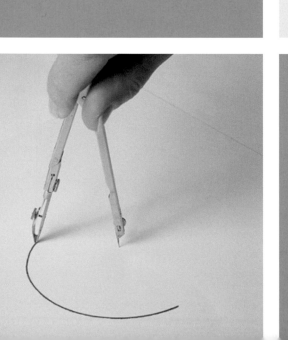

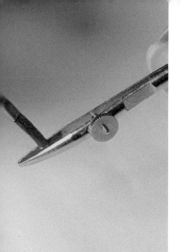

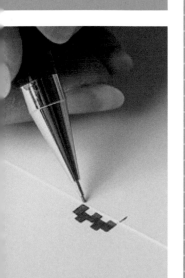

FILLING THE SPACE

The Basics of Layout

For many calligraphy assignments, there are recognized, standard formulas for layout. This is particularly true for certain official documents, certificates, ecclesiastical services, and invitations. Other types of work may also be commissioned with guidelines provided by the client. However, planning the layout—arranging the words to fit the page and determining their size, weight, and style—is still necessary.

The early typefaces mimicked the letterforms developed over many centuries by the scribes. Gutenberg's 42-line Bible illustrates this imitation, which extends to the layout and decoration of the page.

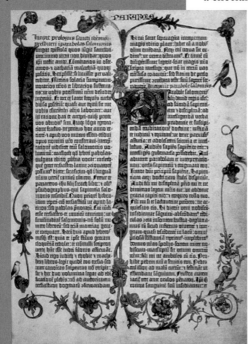

For all layouts, there are many decisions to be made. In order that nothing is overlooked, a good working practice is to draw up a checklist or list of actions. This may cover the following elements of the work:

• heading
• sub-heading
• text
• name of author
• date
• name of calligrapher
• decoration

If the work is an invitation, the list of information includes name, place, date, time, and so on. This list-making, breaking the job down into parts,

helps you to determine the visual and literal importance of each item of information.

Scanning the words will provide more valuable information to contribute to the layout and begin to provide answers to questions. What are the words about? What style of lettering lends itself to the mood or occasion? Who is this for, and who will read it (which may affect size and shape)? Does it need decoration or color? What kinds of materials would be suitable? Where is the piece to be displayed? Is it to be printed or is it a one-off?

MARGINS

The size and shape of the work may not be a foregone conclusion, in which case, you can determine these elements when playing with rough layouts. If the shape is not round, square, or irregular, it will

CREATING MARGINS

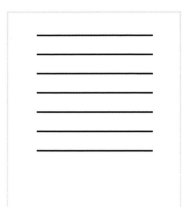

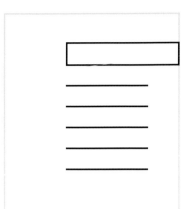

1 One method of achieving a balanced, pleasing layout is to calculate the margins in ratios of 2:2:2:3. In this format, the margins at the top and sides are equal and the base margin is slightly deeper

2 A second ratio for calculating margins is 1½:2:2:4. In this case, the top margin is narrower than the two sides and the base margin is the deepest

3 Modern designs often include text and headings which are positioned "off-center" and may have certain elements that "bleed off" the page. These works may have adjacent margins equal or no margins equal.

be a portrait or landscape rectangle. Margin widths are an important factor in the design. The relationship of the margins to each other will help to balance the entire work. Generally, equal margins around the whole piece do not work well visually. The two most commonly used options are: sides and top of equal depth and the base slightly deeper; or sides of equal proportion, the top slightly less deep and the base deepest of all.

Visual faults occur if the margins are ill considered. Too much surrounding white space will cause the words to be lost, or to appear to float in the center of the page. Unless a small amount of white space is an integral part of the design, the words will

appear cramped and the work poorly conceived. Mounted and framed pictures in a gallery best illustrate traditional proportioning of margins.

Some designs, however, do abandon a regular and properly proportioned margin arrangement. These are designs in which, for example, the color or decoration, or a rule, runs off the page. This is called "bleeding off." This is a perfectly valid solution and can be used very effectively in contemporary works. Look at lots of examples in printed matter—such as books, magazines, advertising leaflets, or posters—and identify how other designers have used this method.

Mastering Spacing

Spacing is obviously very important if you are to be able to arrange text in the way you want over the page. When you have determined the importance of the order of information, and are more familiar with the subject of the text, you may develop a preference for a certain style.

LETTER SPACING

The style of the lettering provides the clue to correct spacing. Some hands are round and open and dictate a need to allow space for the letters to "breathe." Conversely, straight, angular styles, such as some Gothic hands, demand less space. Too much space can make reading uncomfortable and difficult, but so can too little space.

Letter spaces are nearly identical, depending on which letters are adjacent. Aim for a balance between the counter spaces of the letters and the spaces between letters to achieve a balanced rhythm to the whole work.

INTERLINEAR SPACING

Allow enough space between lines of words to ensure that ascenders and descenders do not become entangled. Take particular care if you intend to include flourishing.

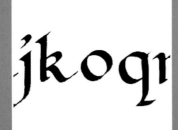

Use the width of an O as a general guide for determining the space between words.

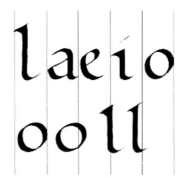

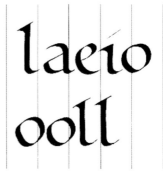

CENTERING TEXT

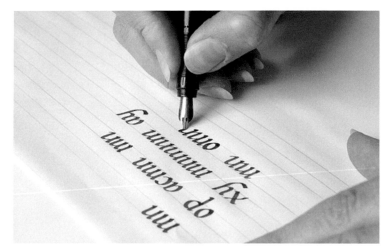

1 Many calligraphic works lend themselves to a centered layout. There are several methods of centering; making up a dummy layout is a quick and accurate way. Begin by transcribing the text in the chosen style and size. Write the text with the correct word spacing and in the individual lines that make up the final piece.

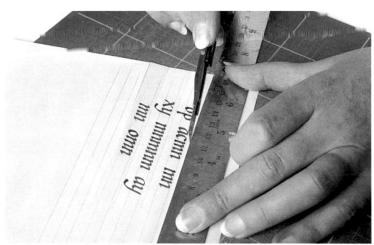

2 Cut out each line as close to the writing as possible. Fold each strip in half so the first and last letters cover each other. The fold marks the center point of the written line. Alternatively, simply measure the halfway point between the outer stroke of the first and last letters and mark this center point very lightly in pencil.

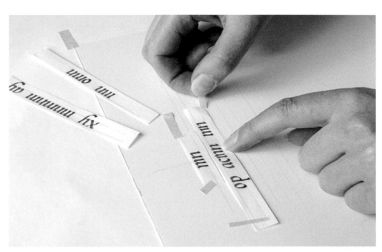

3 On a clean sheet of paper, lightly mark with pencil the vertical centerline. Assemble the strips and align each fold or center mark with the pencil line. Tab each strip into position with masking tape. Pay attention to the space between the strips, especially if a final decision on this space has not yet been reached.

Exploring Alignments

The way in which the lines fall on the page, and whether they are aligned or justified, is an important consideration. There are recognized ways in which this can occur. Centered text is evenly distributed on either side of a centerline. Justified text aligns on both left-hand and right-hand margins. Alternatively, the work can be ranged (aligned) left and ragged (uneven) right, or vice versa, or the lines can form an asymmetrical arrangement.

For all methods of alignment, the rough transcribing of the hand and all the spacing require special attention. If a space is enlarged in the final version, then the line will be, for example, off-center.

There are no rules as to line length; guidelines suggest an average of 66 characters per line

EXPLORING DIFFERENT ALIGNMENTS

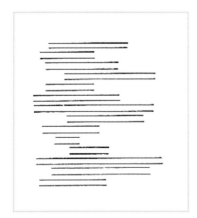

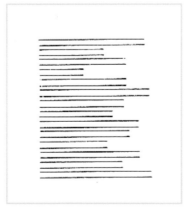

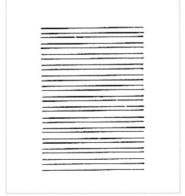

1 An asymmetrical arrangement of lines on the page.

2 On this page the left-hand margin is aligned ("ranged left") and the right-hand margin is unjustified ("ragged right").

3 This text has lines aligned left and right; that is, it is justified left and right.

(character count includes punctuation and word spaces). Practice promotes ability to make visual assessments based on letter size and available space. Vary nib size (alters letter size) and/or space between letters and words. On short lines use line fillers or letter extensions.

DEPTH SCALES

A useful item for ruling up and determining the depth of a work is a depth scale. This provides a practical method of fitting the lines to text. The mathematical formula for determining depth in an evenly spaced work is:

number of lines of text
x
letter height
+
number of interlinear spaces
x
space height.

ASSESSING DEPTH

1 A depth scale is a useful item for ruling up and determining the depth of a piece of work. On the edge of a piece of paper or board, mark the height of the letters as determined by the number of nib widths.

2 Calculate the amount of space required between the lines and mark this on the depth scale. To do this, measure the amount from the base line of the letter height. Starting at the same point on each side of the paper, mark off the line depths and interlinear spaces. Use either pencil or the points of dividers, and keep the marks as close to the edge of the paper as possible.

3 Rule up the writing lines using the marks as a guide. If using a T-square or parallel motion, mark off the line depths on one side of the paper only.

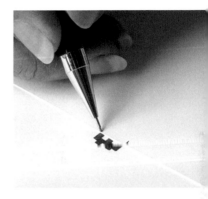

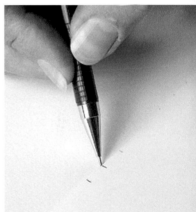

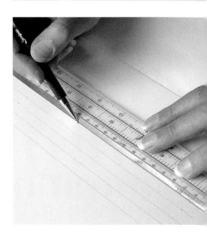

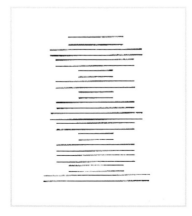

4 A centered arrangement of lines is a pleasing layout for many calligraphic works.

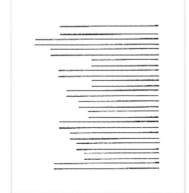

5 Here the "ranged right, ragged left" alignment does not make for easy reading, so is best for short display text.

Composition

Calligraphic design is design of a very specific nature, either predominantly or wholly concerned with the visual arrangement of words. Numerous decisions contribute to the production of a harmoniously arranged work. Some solutions present themselves quite easily, while others are of a more quirky nature.

PLANNING A PIECE

Determine the size of the lettering so that all the information can be fitted. For a poem, select the longest line and use that as a guide when working out the size of the letters. The width of nib used determines the size of the letters, so write out a line using various-sized nibs to get the answer.

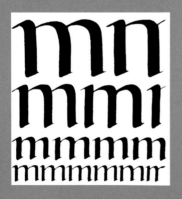

It is advisable to develop a personal checklist of design elements. This will be of enormous benefit, as there are so many considerations that have a serious effect on the final work as a whole. Some resolutions become automatic as your working knowledge develops. If the work is for a client, it is possible that many of the ingredients of the design have been specified already.

READ THE TEXT

Give your attention first to the text or copy. You must establish familiarity and understanding while building a feeling for the words as you read them through. Ask questions as the reading proceeds: what is this about, who will read it, what is important, will it be held or read at a distance? Some solutions will come immediately into focus from the reading, including the purpose and conditions in which the text will be read.

In the early stages, you may have ideas about embellishment— it becomes more obvious whether the text is suitable for flourishing, or whether it should have a border, or perhaps bullet points for highlighting specific and important information. At this stage, such thoughts are merely conjecture and may change, but your first impressions are nevertheless worth noting.

LETTERING

Next, pay attention to the lettering itself: the height, weight, and style must all be determined, and also whether some or all of the letters might be executed in color. In answering the earlier questions, you will already have eliminated some letter styles. From the choices remaining, you can attempt to match the mood and inference of the words.

STYLE

Deciding on the right style for the work is very important. It should be appropriate to the function of the piece: for example, a complicated Gothic hand or flourished letters would be a poor choice for a public notice where immediate legibility is essential.

Remember that you can introduce emphasis with a change to the weight, height, and color of the lettering. For example, a heading written in bold upper-case letters in color will contrast well with a text written in smaller upper- and lower-case letters of the same hand in black. This could make a better design than combining two distinct letter styles. Some changes of height and weight can also create texture and introduce movement.

FINISHED SIZE

The size of the finished work may be predetermined. If it is not, you must focus on the format and dimensions of the piece. First, is it to be landscape or portrait or square? Perhaps it is to be reproduced for an item that will be sent through the post. What sizes of envelopes are available, and is the work to be folded?

The choice of a particular paper or board can often be resolved by the nature of the words to be written. If this is not the case, follow basic rules for selection. Look for color, weight, and surface finish that will complement the calligraphy. All the materials you use are of great

SUBSTRATE SHAPES

1 The final presentation of a work affects how it is received; therefore make the choice of its overall shape an early consideration. The options include portrait: a rectangle with long sides running vertically.

2 The landscape shape is also a rectangle. The long sides are on the horizontal. Work can be placed anywhere in the space. Try experimenting with different layouts, both symmetrical and asymmetrical.

3 The square is the third shape in this group. Work can be arranged to dramatic effect within this geometrically regular figure.

importance. The paper should enhance the work as a whole, but it must also be a sympathetic surface for the chosen medium.

Putting together all of the decisions made so far, you can now proceed with rough workings. Do lots of roughs, nurture the ideas, and learn to trust your intuition. Do not throwaway any scribbles: ironically, the first working is often the best solution.

Headings and Sub-headings

Many factors combine to make a calligraphic design successful. One is the presentation of the work as a whole, and an important contribution to this is the treatment of the heading or title. The role of the heading is multifaceted. The word or group of words has to attract the attention of the viewer to the whole work and to the title itself.

The red words of the title of this work by Paul Shaw are ranged right, an alignment method that requires good planning. The letters of the alphabet have been placed centrally to the work. Here, they are both an illustration and a heading. The names of the authors are treated as sub-heads in size and position of lettering.

Having captured the focus, a heading must allow the reader to read the text. It has, therefore, to stand out and be emphasized in some way. Bold lettering, contrasting colors, good letter spacing, and the careful use of rules or decoration are all effective devices for catching the eye, but in so doing they must not render the information illegible.

HEADING POSITION

The position of the heading is important. In order to make a visual impact on the reader, the words need to be placed slightly apart from the main body of the text. This does not mean that they stand in total isolation; there are several solutions to creating this space apart from just physically separating the title and text.

The first considerations are the size, weight, style, and color of the letters. Then, although the name suggests that a heading should be at the top of a page, this is certainly not the only place, nor, for some works, the best place visually.

The information given by the title is important and must be seen to relate to the whole design. A heading is not an appendage. However, you can experiment with headings in different positions on the page. A single-word title could run vertically down one side of the page. If the text is composed of individual verses or independent pieces of information, the heading could be located in the middle of the page and centered. Alternatively, it could run across the base of the work, be placed at an oblique angle, or be aligned at one side. Look for the solution that offers the most visual impact without loss of meaning.

RESEARCH

Study early and modern examples of calligraphy to see how the problem has been solved before. Observe the variety of solutions and do lots of roughs, working thoroughly through as many options as possible. Mark in the body of the text with lines, ruled if necessary, to indicate the area it will occupy, so you can better perceive the balance of space.

If a heading has not been supplied and one is required, you must give careful thought to the wording. The heading should be thought of as a descriptive statement of the contents of the text, expressed both precisely and succinctly.

If you have to include the name of an author, a date, or a reference relating to the text, consider this at the same time as the heading. Often it is this important data that can create a balanced feel to the work. Do not neglect it; like the heading, it is not an afterthought.

SUB-HEADINGS

It was a relatively common practice of the early scribes to include in their manuscripts one or more lines of words with letters of a smaller size than those of the title, but larger than the text. The words would appear below a heading or after a decorated letter. Usually, they simply formed the beginning of the text, on occasions extending to quite a lengthy introduction. The concept can be most effectively employed and often works particularly well combined with a decorated or dropped capital.

Expert scribes used numerous variations of this arrangement and the best way to understand them is to spend some time looking at the manuscripts. Keeping reference notes and sketches of unusual layouts will help you to expand your repertoire. Although some difficulty may arise in working out the letter size to fit the available space, this practice can make a good contribution to achieving a finely balanced work.

POSITIONING HEADINGS

Headings serve many purposes and their design and placement deserve careful consideration. Experiment with different arrangements on the page to find the most suitable and aesthetically pleasing solution. A grid system may assist in working out the layout of the page.

Most printed matter—books, magazines, and newspapers—is designed using a grid, enabling the designer to align the work in a clean, legible manner, both horizontally and vertically. Look at some examples and see how the text and images are laid out on the page, often in columns of a specific width. Rough sketches are initially sufficient for working out the position of a heading. Once an idea has evolved, begin to work some of the text into the sketches.

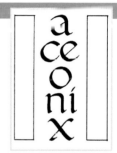

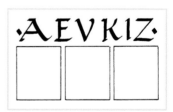

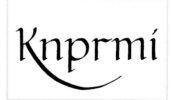

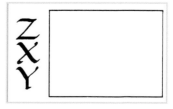

Ruling Lines

The ruling pen is an excellent instrument for drawing up rules of various widths. It can be used with ink or paint, so is versatile for introducing or enhancing work. The pen consists of a handle to which two stainless steel blades are attached. One blade is straight and flat, the other bows slightly outward. The tips of the blades almost meet: the space between them forms a reservoir for ink or paint.

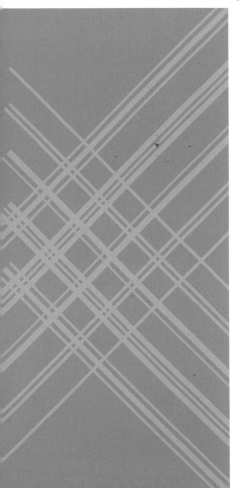

By adjusting a thumbscrew on the bowed blade, you can alter the distance between the blade tips, which dictates the thickness of the line made by the ruling pen.

The medium is loaded into the pen with a brush, or using the dropper supplied with some ink bottles. No ink or paint must be left on the outer edges of the blades, as this could flood the paper if it were to come into contact with the ruler used to guide the pen.

The pen must be operated with both blades resting on the paper. Its movement then discharges the fluid held between the blades.

Although the thickness of the line can be considerably varied by adjusting the pen, some rules may be of a thickness that is best achieved by drawing two parallel lines and filling in between them with a small brush.

A ruling pen attachment is often found in a standard compass set. It can be used in place of the pencil lead normally inserted in the compass, so that you can draw perfect circles of ink or paint.

For fine work, the ruling pen has perhaps been superseded by the technical drafting pen, also available as a compass attachment. However, for the ability to produce rules of different weights and colors, the ruling pen remains unsurpassed.

USING A RULING PEN

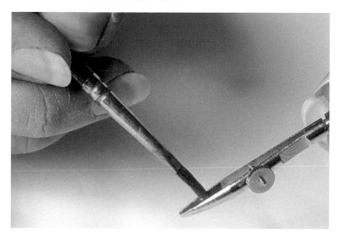

1 Use ink, or paint mixed to a fluid consistency. Insert the color between the blades of the ruling pen with a dropper or brush. Wipe off any excess medium from the edges of the blades.

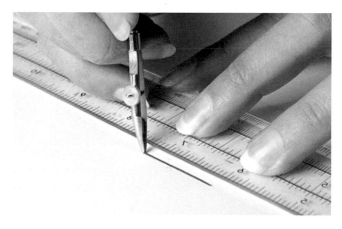

2 Place the ruler flat on the surface with the bevel edge sloping inward and hold firmly. The thumbscrew on the curved blade of the pen should face outward. Hold the pen at a slight angle to the ruler to avoid paint or ink flooding underneath the edge. Keep the drawn stroke light, smooth, and steady, with the points of both blades on the paper to ensure an even flow of medium. It may be necessary to do a "dummy run" to check that the width of the line is correct.

USING A COMPASS

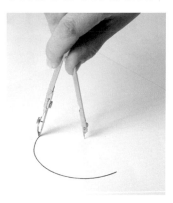

Load the blades of the compass attachment with liquid medium, place the center pin of the compass onto the paper and draw the blades over the surface.

BRUSH RULING

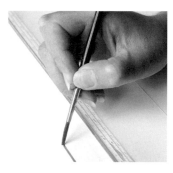

When using a brush to rule lines, avoid smudging by holding the ruler at a 45° angle to the paper so that the edge is not actually touching the paper. Gently draw the brush along the ruler, keeping the ferrule against the ruler's edge to ensure a straight line. Then when the line is completed, remove the ruler carefully to avoid smudging.

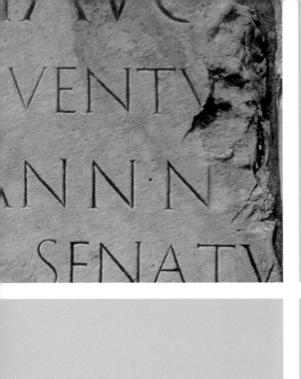

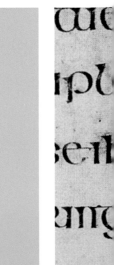

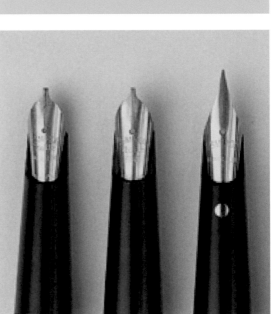

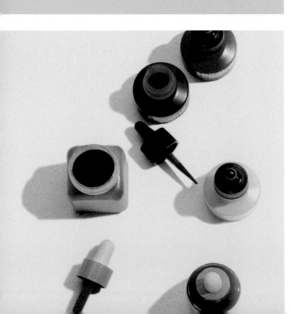

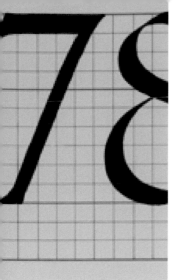

BEFORE
YOU START

Construction of Letters

The term "Roman" is used generally to describe any style appearing in a vertical attitude. When practiced with a quill or square-cut reed pen, instead of being incised on stone monuments, the capitals are known as Quadrata.

UNDERSTANDING LETTER CONSTRUCTION

Do not use too many different letter styles. The advantage of pen lettering is the ability to change the weight and size of the same style to create an impact without introducing a different hand.

To prepare text, transcribe all the words in the chosen style and size onto layout paper. Carefully cut around the words, phrases, and titles, and compose and arrange them on a sheet of paper the same size as the final work.

The capital alphabet contains more straight lines than curves, and many letters have a combination of both vertical and horizontal strokes, giving a squarish appearance—hence the word Quadrata. Since Quadrata is the criterion on which all subsequent styles are based, it is most important to understand this fine, proportioned alphabet. There is an architectural, geometric quality within the style that accounts for the harmony created, especially when lettering is used on buildings in stone.

Capital letters can be defined as having a uniform height throughout; that is, they are written between two parallel lines. The letters are contained without a capital or cap line (top line) and a baseline, with the exception of the letters J and Q which break the baseline in some styles. The lines are also marginally broken by minor optical adjustments to certain letters where pointed apexes and curved strokes slightly overlap.

HEIGHT AND WEIGHT RATIOS

There are now two fixed points, the capital line and the baseline, between which to construct the letters. There is, however, a problem, as you need to decide how far apart the lines should be drawn. Consider the proportions of the letters on page 43. There is a definite relationship between the capital height and the width of the main stroke. In Quadrata, the stem divides into the capital height 10 times, giving a ratio of 1:10. It is important to evaluate this ratio; misinterpretation results in an untrue reproduction of the style.

Once the height and weight ratios have been established, give consideration to the construction

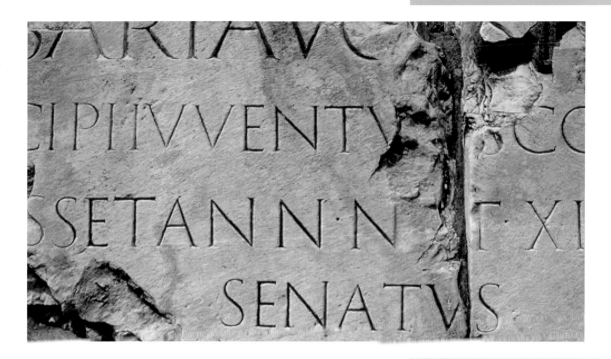

of individual letters. The Romans were a practical and efficient people, and their ability to rationalize and organize is reflected in the formal appearance of their design. The alphabet on pages 44–49 has been produced with a pen and is based on formal Roman characters. If the forms are analyzed, it will be noticed that there are similar characteristics between certain letters—the E, F, and L for example.

It is also apparent that the widths of letters are not identical and that each character occupies a given area in width while retaining a constant height. This width is known as the unit value of the letter, the M and W being the widest, and the I and J the narrowest.

When letters are placed on a gridded square, an immediate visual comparison between the letterforms is possible. The grid illustrated has been divided into units of stem width for convenience, giving an initial square for the capitals subdivided into 10 units of height by 10 units of width. The lower blank portion is for the lower-case letters, which appear after the capitals. The lower portion will then be used to accommodate the descenders.

LOWER CASE AND UPPER CASE

The words "lower case" are a printer's term, now in common use to describe minuscule letters. It derives from the typesetters' custom of storing metal or wooden capital, or majuscule, letters in an "upper" case within easy reach, while the small, or minuscule, letters were stored in a "lower" case. This book uses these more common terms for majuscule and minuscule letters from now onward.

These beautiful incised letters are based on classical Roman forms.

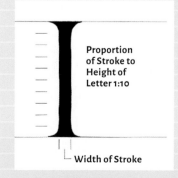

Proportion of Stroke to Height of Letter 1:10

Width of Stroke

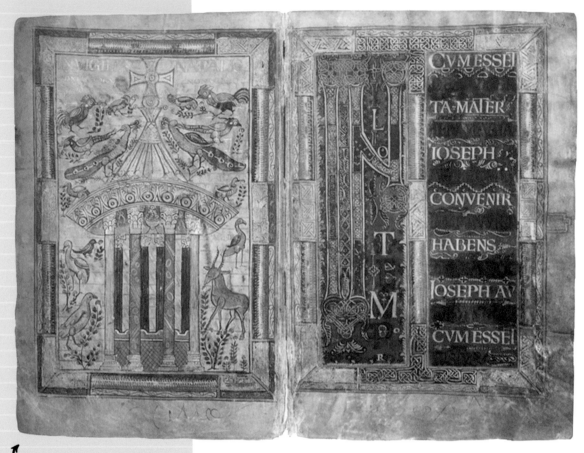

↰ Enlarged Roman capitals decorate
the medieval Godescalc Codex.

ANALYZING LETTERFORMS

When analyzing the construction of individual characters, fix their images firmly in your mind. You will find the proportions of the classical Roman style indispensable as you become more involved with letterforms, and the ability to draw on your experience of this style will help you when analyzing other letterforms.

The alphabet on pages 44–49 has been lettered with a pen to illustrate proportion; it also shows that a classical Roman style can be achieved calligraphically. However, it is not necessarily helpful for you to begin lettering with this style because the construction of the letterforms is not easily reproduced with a square-ended nib. If you wish to letter in this style, within the sample alphabets (see pages 112–119), there is a Roman style for use with the pen.

TERMINOLOGY

In order to understand and analyze letter construction, you need to understand the terminology used to describe the constituent parts of letterforms. There is no standard nomenclature to define constituent parts of letters, but many of the terms are self-explanatory.

The terminology used here is based on that employed by letter designers and therefore may differ from that found in calligraphic references. Many descriptions are repeated from letter to letter as these terms are used generally throughout the alphabet and are not necessarily confined to a specific letter. The parts and names illustrated refer to the Quadrata capitals (majuscule) and a complementary lower-case (miniscule) alphabet, although most of the terms can be employed to define other forms.

A special terminology is used to describe the constituent parts of a letter, such as in this Roman alphabet.

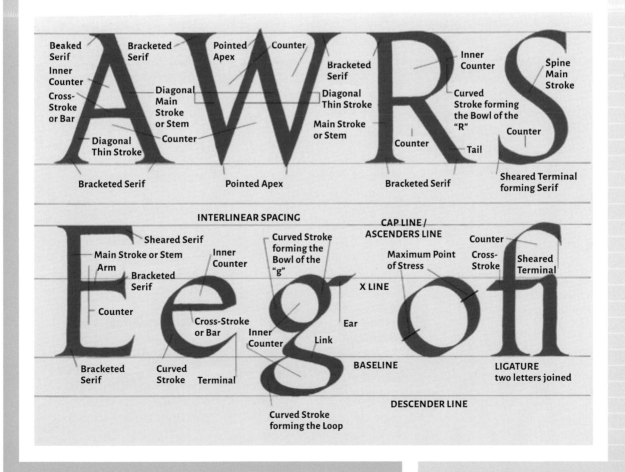

Beaked Serif
Bracketed Serif
Pointed Apex
Counter
Bracketed Serif
Inner Counter
Spine Main Stroke
Inner Counter
Cross-Stroke or Bar
Diagonal Main Stroke or Stem
Counter
Diagonal Thin Stroke
Main Stroke or Stem
Curved Stroke forming the Bowl of the "R"
Counter
Diagonal Thin Stroke
Counter
Tail
Bracketed Serif
Pointed Apex
Bracketed Serif
Sheared Terminal forming Serif

INTERLINEAR SPACING
CAP LINE / ASCENDERS LINE

Sheared Serif
Main Stroke or Stem
Arm
Inner Counter
Curved Stroke forming the Bowl of the "g"
Maximum Point of Stress
Counter
Cross-Stroke
Sheared Terminal
Bracketed Serif
Counter
X LINE
Cross-Stroke or Bar
Inner Counter
Ear
Inner Counter
Link
Bracketed Serif
Curved Stroke
Terminal
BASELINE
LIGATURE two letters joined
Curved Stroke forming the Loop
DESCENDER LINE

Roman Capitals

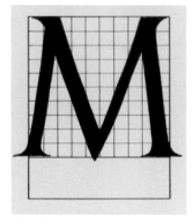 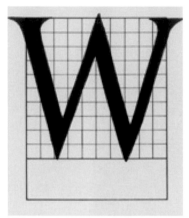

GROUP 1

The M is one of the widest letters of the alphabet, occupying slightly more than the square, with the diagonal strokes breaking the grid at both sides. The true Roman M has pointed apexes, like the A and N, which are easily cut with a chisel; but when a pen or brush is employed, other forms of ending strokes are more natural. The apexes of the M and W (above) end in beaked serifs.

To achieve a pointed apex, the pen strokes end short of the cap and baselines and are then brought to a point. The apexes project beyond the capital and baselines in order to obtain optical alignment with letters ending in square terminals or with beaked or bracketed serifs.

The straight, thin strokes in the M and similar letters are approximately half the thickness of the main stroke; these strokes alter because of the fixed lettering angle of the pen in relation to the direction of the strokes.

The W is perhaps the widest letter of the alphabet. It does not appear in Roman inscriptions but is a medieval addition to the alphabet. In Latin inscriptions, V stood for both the U and V sounds—hence the name "double U," drawn as two Vs joined together, with minor adjustments. The U symbol was a later development, perhaps to avoid confusion.

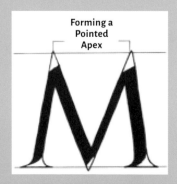

Forming a Pointed Apex

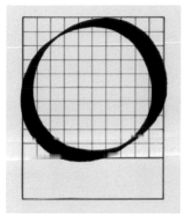

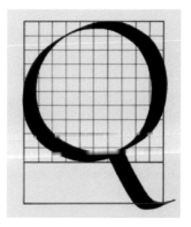

GROUP 2

The O sets the standard for all curved letters and the Q can be said to be an O with a tail. Note well the point at which the tail of the Q joins the curved stroke. Some Qs have a tail that emanates from the lower left-hand curve of the letter as an extension. This is undesirable—the tail should be a separate stroke.

The widest point of the thick stroke of the O is marginally wider than that of the stem of the I. In a free-drawn letter—a letter drawn and then filled in—this is an optical adjustment made to compensate for the tapering or thinning of the stroke toward the thinnest part of the letter. Without this alteration, the curved stroke would appear optically thinner than the stem of the I (see page 49).

In calligraphy, the adjustment to thicken the curved strokes is automatic because of the oblique angle of the pen to the direction of writing. The thin strokes are substantially thinner than half the width of the main stroke, due to this action of the pen. These thin strokes can be thickened to compare more favorably with the straight, thin strokes.

The widest point of the curved stroke is known as the "maximum point of stress" and in the example (right, top) the letter has diagonal stress with oblique shading. There are many styles (right, bottom) that have horizontal stress with vertical shading.

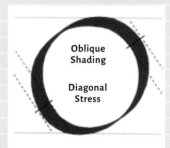

Oblique
Shading

Diagonal
Stress

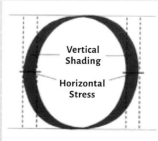

Vertical
Shading

Horizontal
Stress

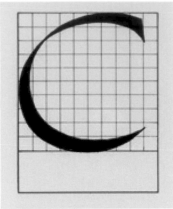

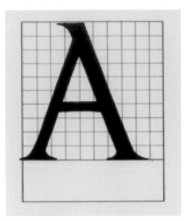

GROUP 3

The C, D, and G take up about nine-tenths of the width of the gridded square. Because they are all rounded forms, the top and bottom curves project slightly over the cap line and baseline. This is to ensure that the round letters appear the same height as those ending in flat serifs. Without this refinement, they would appear smaller.

The C follows the left-hand curve of the O, but the upper and lower arms are somewhat flattened. The upper arm ends in a sheared terminal that is slightly extended to form a beak-like serif. In Quadrata, the lower arm also ends similarly. This serif is extremely difficult to produce with a pen.

G follows the lines of the C, with the G's stem rising from the lower arm to within five-tenths of the letter height, terminating in a bracketed serif. D follows the right-hand curve of the O with the upper and lower curves extending from the initial it is joined with via a curved bracket. The serifs are bracketed on the left hand of the stem.

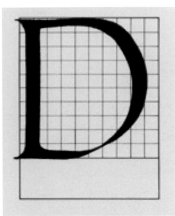

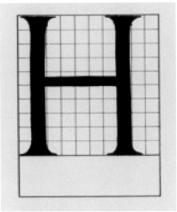

GROUP 4

This is the largest group of letters and includes A, H, K, N, R, T, U, V, X, Y, and Z. All of these letters occupy approximately eight-tenths of the gridded square.

The A, V, X, and Y, being letters formed from triangular elements, should appear almost symmetrical. The V and inverted V shapes should be balanced, and not lean to the right or left.

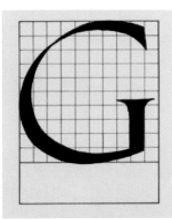

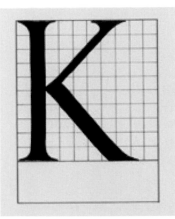

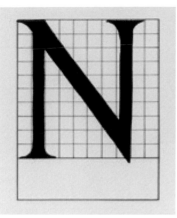 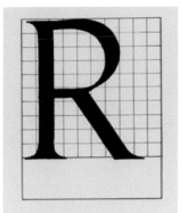

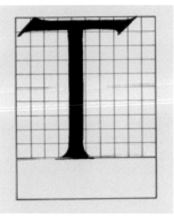 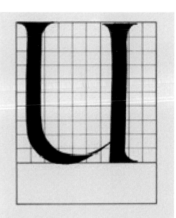

The cross-stroke of the A is positioned midway between the apex and the baseline.

The cross-bar of the H should be slightly above the centerline; otherwise it will seem to be slipping down the main stems.

The two diagonal strokes of the K meet at a point that is also slightly above the center, making the lower counter larger than the upper counter.

The pointed apex of the N should protrude below the baseline, while the upper left-hand serif is beaked.

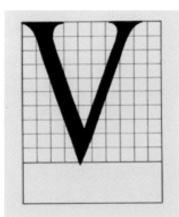

Both the upper part of the bowl of the R and the curved stroke of the U project above the cap line and below the baseline respectively.

The top of the lower cross-stroke that joins the bowl of the R is positioned on the centerline.

A careful note should be made as to where the tail of the R meets the bowl.

The cross-bar of the T is sheared to the lettering angle on the left and right sides, ending in a slight serif. The spurs added to the serifs protrude above the cap line.

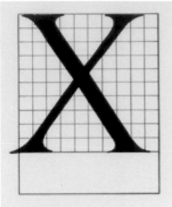

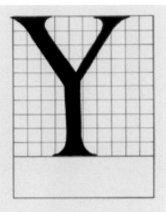

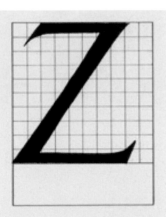

The Z is a problem letter in this alphabet because the main diagonal stem requires a change of pen angle to thicken the stroke.

Otherwise, the stem appears as a hairline-thin stroke. This makes Z difficult to execute with the pen.

GROUP 5

Within this group are the letters B, E, F, L, P, and S, each letter occupying approximately half the width of the gridded square.

The upper bowl of the B is smaller than the lower and therefore the intersection is above the centerline. This is intentional: if both bowls were equal in size, the letter would appear top-heavy.

The upper arm of the E is slightly longer than the middle arm, which is placed high on the centerline, making the upper counter smaller than the lower. Again this is optically necessary. The lower arm projects a little beyond the upper arm, with both ending in sheared, bracketed serifs.

The F may be regarded as an E minus the lower arm. The L is an E without the upper arms. The stem at the cap line has the addition of a bracketed serif on the right.

The letter P at first glance resembles a B minus the lower bowl. Closer inspection will show that the bowl is larger than the upper bowl of B. The cross-stroke joins the bowl to the stem below the centerline.

The upper counter of the S is smaller than the lower counter, with the letter sloping slightly to

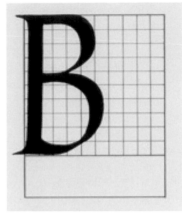

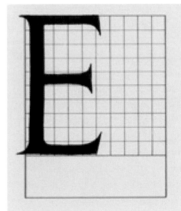

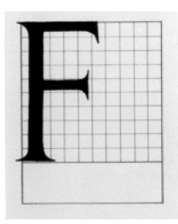

the right. The diagonal spine is of uniform thickness until it tapers to meet the curved arms. The S is a diagonally stressed letter, having this characteristic in common with the A, K, M, N, R, V, W, and, in this alphabet, Z (which is the only letter with a thick diagonal stroke running from top right to bottom left).

The upper and lower arms of S end in sheared terminals and fractionally extend to form beak-like serifs. It is important for balance that the lower counter is slightly larger than the upper counter. This gives the S a slight forward tilt, making it one of the most challenging letters in which to achieve a good poise.

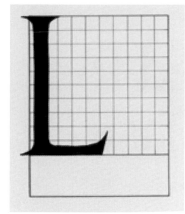

GROUP 6

The I and J take up approximately three-tenths of the gridded square. The I sets the standard for the alphabet in height and stem width.

The J does not appear in the inscription on the Trajan Column where its present-day sound is represented by an I. J is written like an I minus the baseline bracketed serif, where the stroke continues through the

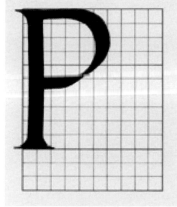

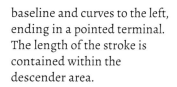

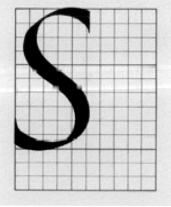

baseline and curves to the left, ending in a pointed terminal. The length of the stroke is contained within the descender area.

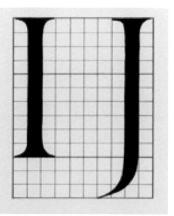

The Need for a Lower Case

The Quadrata and Rustica capitals were followed by Uncial, born of the need to write more quickly while still maintaining a formal style. Uncial is a true pen form with a simple construction and comparatively clean finishing strokes. Uncial was the literary hand for fine books from the fifth to the eighth centuries. The letterforms were more rounded than traditional Roman capitals.

An example of Uncial and Half-uncial lettering from the *Book of Kells*.

The chief characteristic letters within the style were the A, D, E, H, and M and, although they were still written between the capital and baselines, certain letters, namely the D, F, G, H, K, L, P, Q, X, and Y, began to have longer stems that marginally broke through the cap line and baseline.

Uncial was followed by Half-uncial and here some letters are predominantly seen to break through the writing lines forming ascender and descender areas. Letterforms were modified, notably the a, b, e, g, and l, with the remaining letters receiving only minor amendments, if any at all.

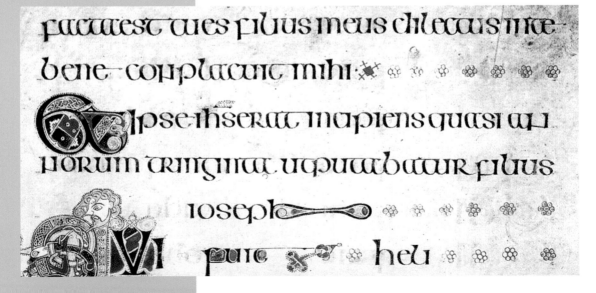

Half-uncial led the way for other minuscule scripts to be developed.

Toward the end of the eighth century, with the revival of learning, came a reform of the hand in which works of literature were to be written. Emperor Charlemagne, who governed a vast area of Europe, commissioned the abbot and teacher Alcuin of York to rationalize and standardize the various minuscule scripts that had developed. Alcuin studied the former styles of Quadrata, Rustica, Uncial, and Half-uncial and developed a new minuscule as a standard book style. This has become known as the Carolingian minuscule after its instigator, Charlemagne. Calligraphy now entered a new era with this distinctive true pen form.

Although the Romans used mainly capital letterforms, a classical lower-case alphabet, together with Arabic numerals, has been included here to complement the capital forms previously described and to give you an insight into their construction. The letters and numerals that follow are of classical proportions and, once their relative widths and construction details have been mastered, knowledge of them will stand you in good stead for lettering the sample alphabets in this book.

The letters have been placed on a grid that consists of squares of stem width: 13 units deep, with four units allocated for the ascenders (those letters that reach the cap or ascender line—the h for instance), six units for the x-height (that

portion of the grid that contains letters such as the s), and three units below the x-height (to accommodate the descenders of letters such as the g and y). The characters have been grouped together with common widths, starting with the widest and ending with the narrowest.

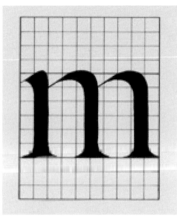
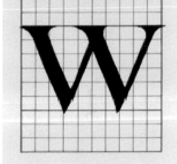

GROUP 1

The lowercase m and w occupy approximately 10 units, and both letters are contained within the x-height. In the m, observe the point at which the curved shoulder of the second stroke meets the stem of the first—the second shoulder intersects at the same height. The serif of the first stroke and both shoulders, because they are curved, are positioned to break the x line, giving optical alignment with the letters v, w, x, y, and z. Their tops are either bracketed serifs or, in the z, a cross-stroke.

The m is not an n joined with another n, as the inner counters of the m are narrower than that of the n. The apexes of the w extend slightly below the baseline; the inner apex is the x line. This shows that the diagonal strokes are positioned correctly.

dghkn

pquxy

GROUP 2

Each letter in this group occupies about seven units. The group comprises d, g, h, k, n, p, q, u, x, and y. There are three letters with ascenders (d, h, and k), four letters with descenders (g, p, q, and y), and three contained within the x-height.

In the d, at the point where the lower curve of the bowl meets the main stem, there should be a triangular space formed by the upward movement of the curved stroke. The upper serif of the main stem projects slightly above the ascender or cap line.

The old-style g is very challenging. In this style, the bowl does not take up the whole depth of the x-height: instead it occupies just over three units. It then joins the link that carries down to the baseline and then turns sharply to the right and ends forming the right side of the loop. The loop is accommodated within the three-unit descender area. The ear is attached to the bowl at the right side, leaving a v-shaped space.

The h and n are formed in a similar fashion, although the h has the first stem lengthened to form the ascender, with the serif extending over the ascender line. The letter n can be taken as an h without the ascender. The ascender stem of the k is like the h, with the diagonal thin stroke and the tail intersecting just above the centre of the x-height.

With the p, the join of the lower part of the bowl to the stem is somewhat flattened. A serif is attached to the bowl at the top left-hand corner. The q is not a p in reverse but is totally different in character, having no serif at the x line and with the upper stroke of the bowl being straightened to meet the stem.

Similarly the u is not an inverted n. The upper serifs protrude beyond the x line and a space is left where the curve makes its upward movement to meet the second stem. In the x, the point of intersection of the thin and thick strokes is above the x-height center, making the lower counter larger than the upper. The diagonal thick stroke of the y does not reach the baseline but is intersected by the thin stroke, which follows through to the descender line, where it ends in a flat, bracketed serif.

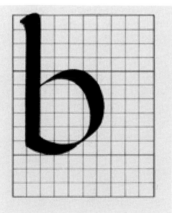

GROUP 3

The two letters in this group take up approximately six-and-a-half units in width. The b is an ascending letter, the main stem swinging to the right before it meets the baseline. The O is contained within the x-height, with the exception of minor optical adjustments at the x line and baseline.

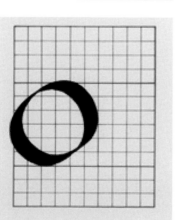

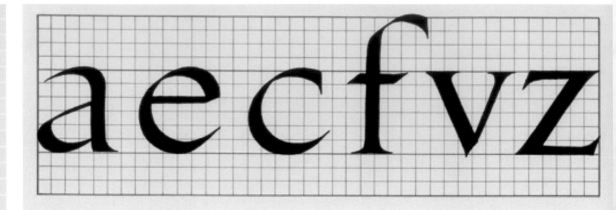

GROUP 4

This group contains the a, c, e, f, v, and z, and, with the exception of the f, they are all contained within the x-height.

The a starts from a pointed, curved arm that leads into the main stem. The bowl starts from the stem above the centerline of the x-height and moves to the left before the downward curve. It rejoins the stem above the baseline, leaving a triangular shape. The letter c follows the left-hand stroke of the O, the upper arm being straightened slightly and ending in a sheared terminal that is extended to

form a beak-like serif. The lower arm ends in a pointed terminal. The e follows the c; the upper arm is not straightened but flows round. The stroke ends obliquely. The bowl is formed by a cross-stroke that is positioned above the x-height center.

The f is an ascending letter, starting its main stroke below the ascender line with the arm projecting to the right and ending in a sheared, beak-like serif. The cross-bar is positioned just below the x line. The v and z both follow exactly the same construction as their capital counterparts.

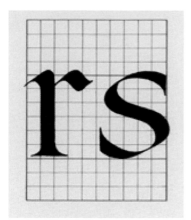

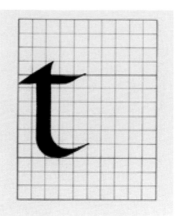

GROUP 5

This grouping contains three characters, about five units wide: the r, s, and t. From the main stem of the r, there is a small shoulder stroke that should not be overdone—if it is too long, it can interfere with the lettering of the character that follows. The s is constructed in the same manner as its capital. The main stem of the t starts obliquely, a little way above the x line, moving to the right before reaching the baseline and ending in a pointed terminal. Like the f, the cross-stroke is finished with a slight upward movement.

GROUP 6

The i, j, and l fall into this narrow-letter group. They are easily constructed, with the humble i and j setting the pattern for straight letters. The dot over the i and j can be round or flat and is usually positioned about midway between the x and ascender lines. The j initially follows the i but extends below the baseline, where it curves to the left, ending in a pointed terminal.

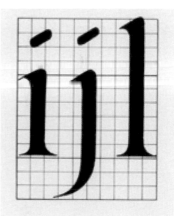

Numerals

The Romans used letters of the alphabet for their numeric reference. We are all familiar with the Roman-style numerals applied to a clock face, but perhaps not so with M = 1,000, D = 500, C = 100, and L = 50. It takes little imagination to see that mathematical calculations could be made easier by changing the symbols. The Arabs did exactly that and based their system on 10 numeric signs, the "Arabic numerals" we use today.

They can be either of uniform height ("lining numerals") or of varying height ("old style" or "hanging numerals"). In the latter style, the 1, 2, and 0 appear within the x-height, the 6 and 8 are ascending numerals, and the 3, 4, 5, 7, and 9 are descending characters.

The main characteristics of the numerals need little explanation, but a few points should be noted. For example, if numerals are not constructed carefully they can appear to be falling over. This is because they are mainly asymmetric in form, with the exception of the 0, 1, and 8, which are basically balanced.

If the curve of the 2 is allowed to project beyond the base cross-stroke, it will appear to be leaning to the right. If the tail of the 9 is not carried sufficiently far to the left, the figure will appear to lean to the left; if too far, it will look as if it is leaning to the right. The 9 is not an

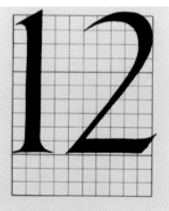

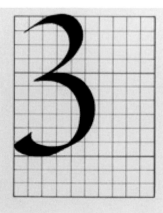

inverted 6. The join of the small curved stroke to the main curved stem alters in each case, making the inner counters slightly different in shape.

The upper counters of the 3 and 8 should be smaller than the lower one, otherwise the characters will be top heavy. The cross-bar of the 4 is fairly low on the stem so that the inner counter does not appear too small.

The diagonal stroke of the 7 cannot extend too far to the left: once it goes beyond the alignment of the upper stroke, it makes the letter look as if it were leaning backward. If the cross-stroke of the 5 is too long, it too can appear to lean to the right.

Finally, note that the numeral 0 is compressed and not a letter O.

The character & is known as the ampersand. This is possibly a corruption of the mixed English and Latin phrase "and per se and." It is an ancient monogram of the letters e and t, the Latin word *et* meaning "and." The *et* in this instance is not reflected in the character on the grid, which occupies nine units in width.

The upper bowl is much smaller than the lower, with the angle of the diagonal stroke cutting through to form a semicircular counter and the tail ending in a bracketed serif. The upward tail to the bowl ends with a bracketed serif above the centerline.

SYMBOLS

Within our written language, there are many other symbols, such as parentheses, exclamation marks, and question marks, to name but a few. These will become natural enough to create once you start practicing calligraphy.

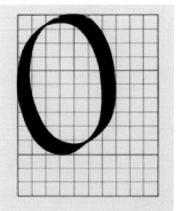
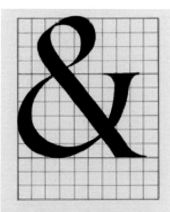
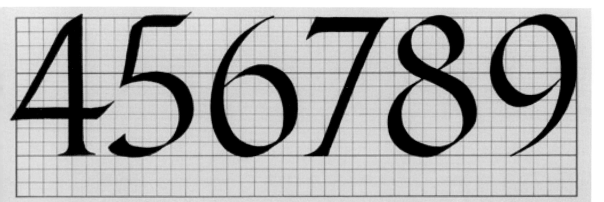

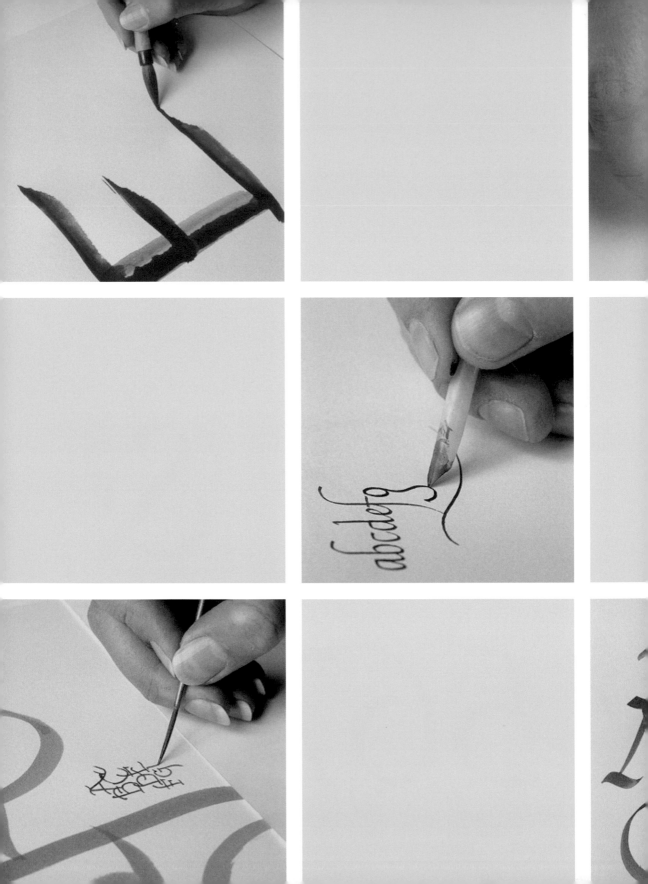

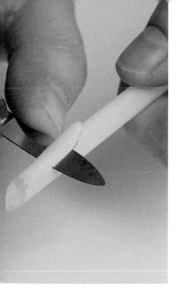

CORE
TECHNIQUES

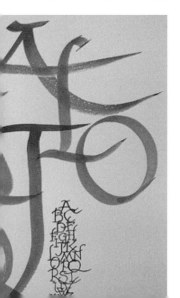

Pen Practice

It is the angle of the nib in relation to the direction of writing and the width and weight of stroke that gives the letterforms their characteristics. A style that is formed with the nib angle at 30° to the writing line will have a different visual appearance to that lettered at 45°. This is because it is the angle that determines the weight of each stroke and the stress of the round letters.

B ecause the pen angle is 30°, a vertical stroke will only be as wide as the image the nib makes at that angle, and not equivalent to the full nib width. In a round letterform, there is a point at which the whole of the nib width is used, due to the pen traveling in a semicircle.

The maximum width of stroke—"the stress"—is exactly 90° to the thinnest stroke, which is fortunate for round letterforms because, if the nature of the tool used did not produce this automatically, round letterforms would appear thinner than vertical ones of the same weight.

Indeed, when letterforms are freely constructed with a pencil and then filled in with a brush, the curved, thick strokes are increased in weight to provide an optical balance with straight strokes.

The weight of the stroke is determined by the angle of the pen and the direction of travel. Diagonal strokes vary in weight, depending on the direction of the stroke. Strokes made from top left to bottom right are more consistent than those formed top right to bottom left. Horizontal strokes are of a uniform width. These variations are acceptable in pen lettering and give the forms a natural, unforced appearance. The alphabet is constructed from common vertical, horizontal, diagonal, and curved strokes.

Letterforms within the alphabet have common likenesses and, although there are 26 characters, the strokes that are repeated within the capitals and lower cases are frequent. This repetition makes the task easier: once the basic strokes used in letter construction have been

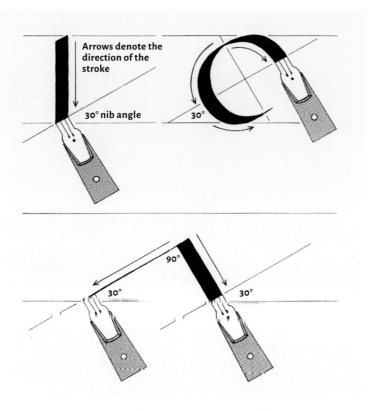

Arrows denote the direction of the stroke

30° nib angle

30°

90°

30°

30°

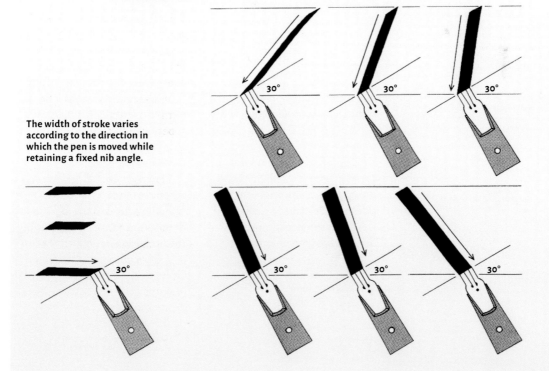

30°

30°

30°

The width of stroke varies according to the direction in which the pen is moved while retaining a fixed nib angle.

30°

30°

30°

30°

mastered, the forming of individual letters is a relatively simple matter.

The ability to produce the strokes with confidence comes from practicing them many times on layout paper.

FORMING STROKES

Unlike handwriting, where the pen is lifted from the paper only occasionally between words or necessary breaks in form, calligraphic lettering dictates that the pen is lifted after each stroke. This is because it is the combination of strokes that creates the letterforms.

The pen is nearly always used with a pulling action toward the letterer. Horizontal strokes are made from left to right. The nib should glide across the sheet with just enough pressure to keep it in contact with the writing surface.

It is at this point that the newcomer to calligraphy is often faced with problems. It is essential that the pen angle be maintained while producing the stroke, whatever direction is taken. This usually takes all a calligrapher's concentration and can result in the nib not being in contact with the paper throughout the movement. This skipping will cause an uneven weight in the stroke, and the result is likely to be patchy.

Control over the pen for small letters is achieved with the fingers for the up-and-down movements, with the wrist being used only a little for rounded letters. When forming larger letters, on the other hand, say over $^3/_4$ in (20mm), the movement comes from the shoulder, with the whole arm moving down the writing surface. The height of the letter, at which the transition from finger to arm movement is made, is dependent on the dexterity of the individual. So the exercise requires mainly finger and wrist action with, perhaps, some of the longer, diagonal strokes needing arm movement. The third and little finger rest on the paper all the time, and help to support the pen holder.

BASIC LETTER STROKES

Begin by tracing over the forms given in the exercise (right). You need a nib of the same size used here. To test this, take a nib and compare it with the nib and width of stroke marked at the side of the sample exercise. It is better if the size can be matched exactly, although a small variation will not matter at this stage.

The main aim of the exercise is for the student to become familiar with the action of the pen, and to develop a rhythm when forming the images.

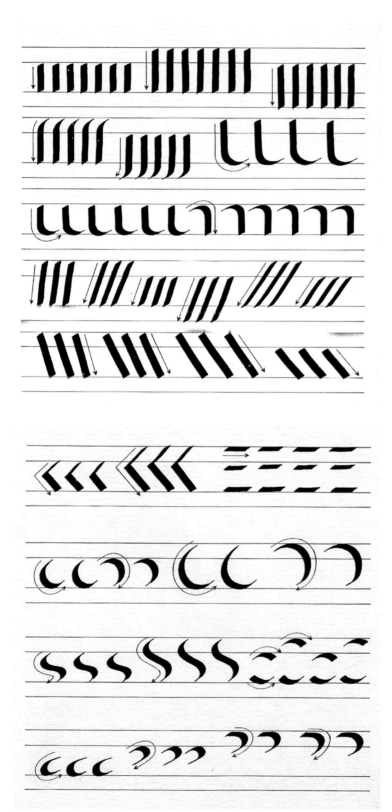

These simple strokes form the basis of letter construction.

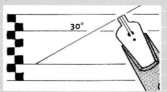

30°

Making a Quill Pen

The quill pen, which has been in use for over two thousand years, remains unsurpassed for some of its excellent qualities. This extraordinary tool was developed at the same time as vellum became the preferred substrate, being of superior quality to papyrus. The development of the formal Roman capital alphabet demanded a flexible writing implement with the ability to produce fine lines.

USING A QUILL PEN

The quill can produce both fine and thick lines, as required for calligraphy.

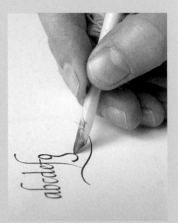

The characteristics of the quill pen enabled scribes to write legibly and to establish a rhythm producing good letter shapes.

Variations in preparing the quill nib influenced the hands for which it was used. The nib could be cut at a variety of angles, or sharpened to a very fine point. The angle of the pen altered the strokes and the forms described here. Instruction books were made, containing illustrations of how to hold the quill pen and its angle of manipulation. There are fine engravings showing a scribe manipulating a chunky instrument; this is the quill pen. Some pictorial references show the barbs of the feather intact, but in fact this is not convenient for writing. There are many excellent sources of quills; the primary flight feathers of geese, swans, and turkeys are ideal. For delicate work, crow and duck quills provide a very fine shaft.

The natural curve of the quill is important, so that the instrument sits comfortably in the hand. Left-handed calligraphers should select quills from the right side of the bird, and right-handed calligraphers from the left.

PREPARING THE QUILL

The quill must be thoroughly dried out before it can be cut for use to eliminate the oils. It may take months to do this naturally, so substitute a brief exposure to a source of gentle artificial heat.

Heating alters the quill from its original opaque soft-textured form to a harder, clarified shaft.

The method of applying heat needs to produce the right flexibility and hardness. One simple way is to position the

CUTTING A QUILL

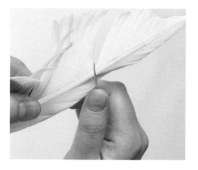

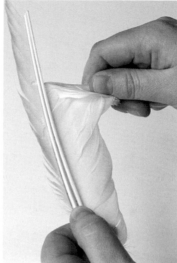

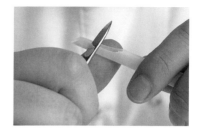

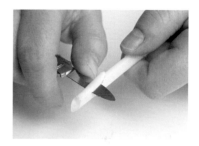

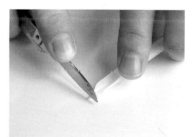

1 Strip the barbs from the shaft. Using the back of a penknife, scrape the length of the barrel to remove the outer membrane. Rub the shaft with a rough cloth.

2 Before cutting, the quill must be hardened and clarified. First, cut off the sealed end of the barrel, then soak the quill in water overnight. The next morning, heat some silver sand in a shallow tray or pan. Take the quill from the water and shake it vigorously. Using a long point, such as a knitting needle, push the "coil" inside the quill to the end. Spoon hot sand into the barrel and, when it is full, plunge it into heated sand for a few seconds. Then cut the top off the quill.

3 Make an oblique cut, long and slanting, downward to the tip of the quill.

4 Make another oblique cut below the first to shape the shoulders of the quill. This gives the familiar stepped arrangement of the shoulders and nib tip. Remove any pith remaining in the shaft. Make a small slit in the shaft to aid the flow of ink down to the writing tip. Do this very carefully: a length of $1/4$ in (6mm) is adequate.

5 Work on a smooth, hard surface, such as glass, for the final sharpening. Place the nib underside uppermost. Make a clean cut down the nib tip in a single motion. Pare the topside of the nib finely to complete the quill.

quill about 2in (5cm) above a hotplate and rotate it slowly for about 10 seconds. After heating, scrape off the greasy membrane from the outside and remove the pith from inside; then polish the quill. Next, cut it to a length of 7–8in (18–20cm). Shape the quill nib with a scalpel or a sharp steel knife.

To maintain writing quality, the nib then can be retrimmed as often as necessary. If it is used often, the nib will need to be re-cut.

Now you are ready to use a brush to load the quill pen with ink, and begin to write.

Using a Reed Pen

Reed pens, which were among the earliest forms of nibbed writing instruments, were commonly used by Middle Eastern scribes because of the plentiful supply of sturdy and suitable reeds in their part of the world. The Egyptians, too, made reed pens and soft reed brushes for writing on papyrus. The Romans, having adopted the use of papyrus, found the reed pen a most suitable instrument with which to write.

It was sometimes referred to as a "calamus," after the particular species of palm that provided the raw material. Cut to shape, the reed pen was used to apply ink to parchment and linen as well as papyrus.

MAKING A REED PEN

A reed pen can be made quite easily and certainly cheaply. Garden cane is the most common equivalent to the original types of reed. The hollow cane is easily cut to length and shaped, using a sharp knife, to form a writing nib.

Inspect the cane carefully to make sure it has no splits or imperfections that could result in any number of disasters when you start using it to write. Cut it to a manageable length—8in (20cm) is recommended.

WRITING WITH A REED PEN

The cane, being nothing but a hollow tube, provides an excellent reservoir for ink. Take care not to let it flood the writing, though; work on a flat or slightly inclined surface. Like most calligraphic implements, it resists a pushing motion—you obtain the best results from pulling the stroke.

In comparison with the quill, the reed pen has less flexibility. It cannot sustain such fine and accurate shaping, and the overall effect of work written with this pen may not be as eloquent. It does have excellent qualities, however, that make it a valid implement for many styles of writing. The calligrapher can select canes of different sizes and prepare a varied range of nib widths accordingly. The resulting bold letterforms are

USING A REED PEN

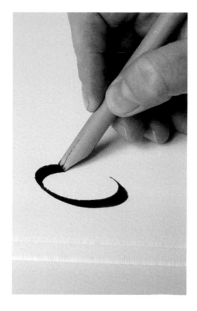

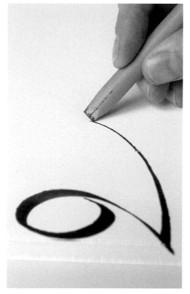

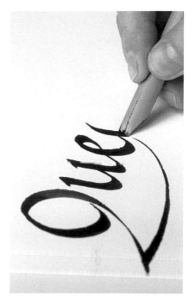

1 A reed pen has a different "feel" from a metal-nibbed pen; because it is made all in one piece, it feels almost like an extension of your hand and is very pleasurable to use. The width of the strokes made with a reed pen is dictated by how wide the nib has been cut. This illustration demonstrates the firm and solid strokes that this simple instrument is capable of producing.

2 The reed pen has the ability to produce both the extremely fine lines and the thick strokes required for calligraphy. Holding the reed pen at the prescribed pen angle, a fine line is extended from the tail of the letter. To complete the line the right-hand side of the nib is lifted off the paper, and the left-hand side of the nib drags wet ink into a hairline.

3 The lower-case letters are written confidently, and show how a nib made from an inflexible material can produce very well the familiar characteristics of calligraphy.

4 When working with a reed pen, always keep the top side of the nib clean. Take care not to overload with ink, as this could result in blotting or smudging. This example shows an excellent balance between thin and thick strokes, and a fine hairline extension to the last letter. This last was achieved by dragging wet ink with the left-hand corner of the nib.

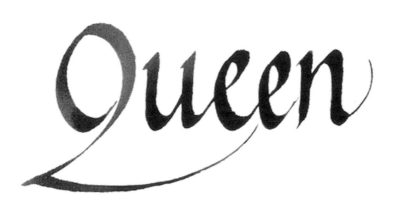

highly effective in poster work, headings, and titles, and can be matched to specific "one-off" jobs where a particular nuance is sought.

The Romans used the reed pen in the execution of their square capitals and rustic hands. The method of holding the pen between the index and middle

MAKING A REED PEN

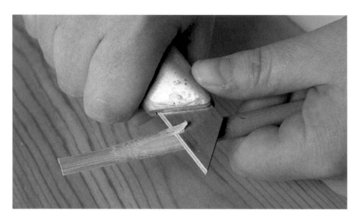

1 Assemble the materials—a suitable reed or cane, a sharp knife, and a hard surface on which to cut. Soak the reed or cane for at least 15 minutes, then cut it with a sharp knife while it is still wet. Cut the cane to a comfortable working length —about 8in (20cm). The first cut, shown here, is an oblique slash down toward one end.

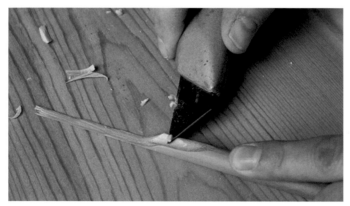

2 Shape the shoulders of the nib. Then, using the point of the knife, clean out any pith inside the cane that has been exposed by the first cut.

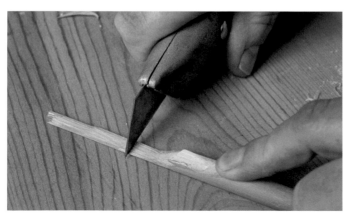

3 Firmly hold the pen on the cutting surface and trim the end to nearer the eventual nib length. Turn the pen through 90° and make a small slit down the center of the nib, at right angles to the writing edge.

fingers must have influenced the way Rustica letters evolved, with thin uprights and thick cross strokes. Other variations occurred with these letterforms, including a slight pull to the right in curved strokes and a condensing of the overall shape, especially when compared with the roundness of Roman capitals.

4 If the nib seems too thick, very carefully pare it down to make it thinner. Holding the nib underside up, make a vertical cut across the nib end.

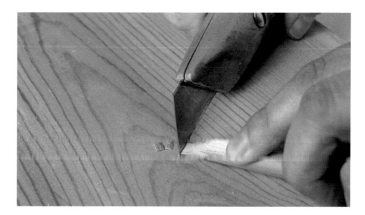

5 Make a small diagonal cut on the upper side of the nib, down toward the end. This will produce a fine writing edge.

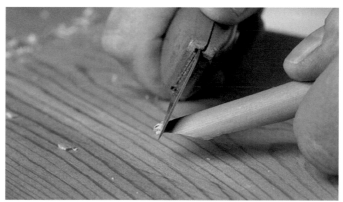

6 The reed pen is now ready to use. A brush is used to transfer ink onto the underside of the nib.

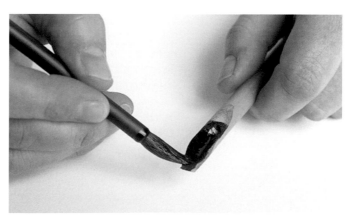

Brush Lettering

Brushes are excellent tools for practice and experimentation.
The ability to use different brushes and a variety of inks and
paints is a great asset, providing a range of instant visualizations.
The best way to learn the possibilities of brush lettering is to
work on quite a large scale and freely, in an informal style.

REVERSING OUT

Calligraphy, with its strong patterns of black and white, lends itself well to reproduction in print. A work designed for reproduction in black on white, or on a color, can be given further dimension by reversing out part of the design. This can be done as artwork by hand, but it is easier to submit the piece to be reversed out as finished artwork in black on white to a printer, who will do it photographically in the darkroom. Further interest can be added by having part of the design—a box or rule, for example—bleeding off the page.

A "hidden agenda" exists when working with brushes: particularly when the ink or paint on the brush diminishes, resulting in interesting textural contrasts. For example, if the ink runs dry in mid-letter, you can make a positive feature of the change of emphasis, rather than dispensing with the work.

Experiment by placing wet, different colors side by side and letting them merge. Planning the color selection can produce exciting and interesting results.

Broad, flat, or square-cut brushes produce bold lettering. Manipulation of the brush angle, particularly for a horizontal stroke, creates further interest.

When working with brushes, you will soon realize that, having found a successful solution in rough form, recreating the exact same image in the finished work is not easy. Try to regard this as an exciting challenge, not as a deterrent. Because of the free movement of the brush, a good understanding of letter shapes will be essential to achieving convincing lettering.

Discovering which brush achieves the required impact is truly a matter of trial and error. Favorite solutions will reveal themselves to you, so get to know the marks of as many brushes as possible. The traditions of Eastern calligraphy are founded in the use of brushes, the hairs of which come to a fine point, making different marks from those of square-cut brushes. Your attempts at lettering with pointed brushes may result in images related to Oriental brush-writing styles. Study of Eastern brush techniques will make an enriching addition to your repertoire.

ARRANGING LETTERS

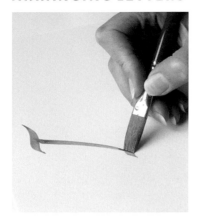

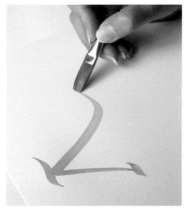

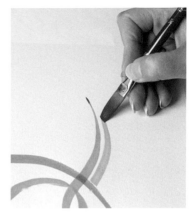

1 Working with a large square-cut brush permits much freedom of individual expression. The first letter provides an anchor from which the remaining letters can hang, or around which they can be grouped.

2 The letters are constructed in the traditional manner of following a stroke sequence. The brush is held at an angle either suitable to the chosen style of lettering or to produce the intended weight of stroke for a particular piece.

3 Pleasing arrangements can be arrived at, often unintentionally, when practicing lettering with a brush. An extended stroke to create a swashed letter is increasingly accomplished with a brush.

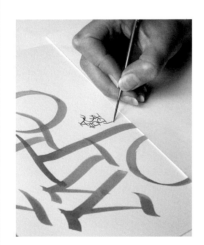

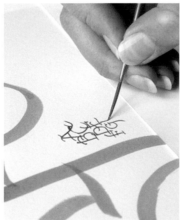

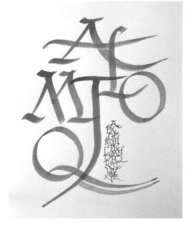

4 Place a sheet of clean paper under your writing hand to keep the writing surface clean and free of grease. Allowing the design to grow, without adhering to any preconceived ideas, often produces pleasing results.

5 The introduction of a second color and a different weight of letter provides two immediate contrasts. Delicate strokes made with a fine-pointed brush further contrast with the weight of broad strokes made with a flat brush.

6 The completed piece illustrates contrasts of color, letter size, and style. Consideration has been made of the space occupied by the freely written individual letters and of their collective arrangement.

Brush lettering can be incorporated in a wide range of designs, creating strong visual effects with an enticing air of informality. For example, a brush-lettered headline next to the more formal writing of the metal nib is very effective.

In this role, brush lettering played a major part in the advertising design of the 1930s and 1940s, particularly in the United States. If you look at examples of advertising design from that period, you will see the potential of using freely written brush script with formal typeset copy.

USING A POINTED BRUSH

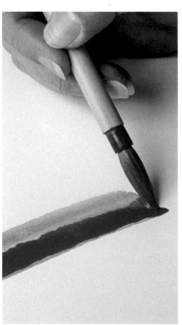

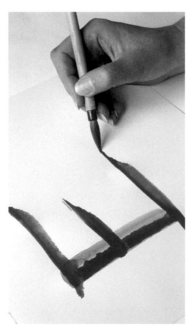

1 A pointed brush, of the kind used for Chinese calligraphy, is excellent for practicing freely constructed letters. Chinese brushes are designed to hold much more paint or ink than a traditional Western watercolor brush.

2 Chinese brushes are also versatile: fine strokes can be produced with the tip, and broad strokes with the body.

EXPLORING SINGLE LETTER SHAPES

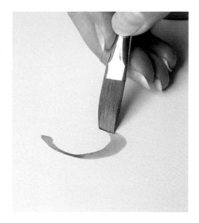

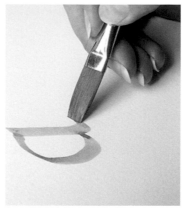

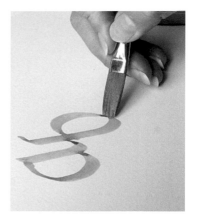

1 Practicing single letter shapes with a large square-cut brush provides an excellent method for learning about letter construction.

2 The sequence of stokes that make up the letters is the same as that used with a pen.

3 Using a brush provides a flexibility of physical approach not available with other instruments. The springiness and lightness of touch of the brush hairs on the page, compared with the rigidity of a steel nib, allow much freedom of movement across the page.

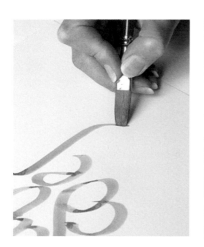

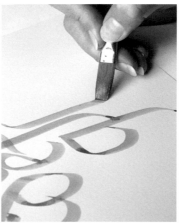

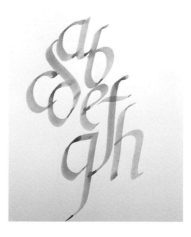

4 The opportunity to dispense with the confines of guidelines is a chance to experiment with offsetting letters on the page.

5 The head of the brush is kept at a consistent angle to enable thin and thick strokes to be formed.

6 Even if some of the letters do not "feel" right, do not abandon the piece: the purpose here is simply to practice manipulating the brush.

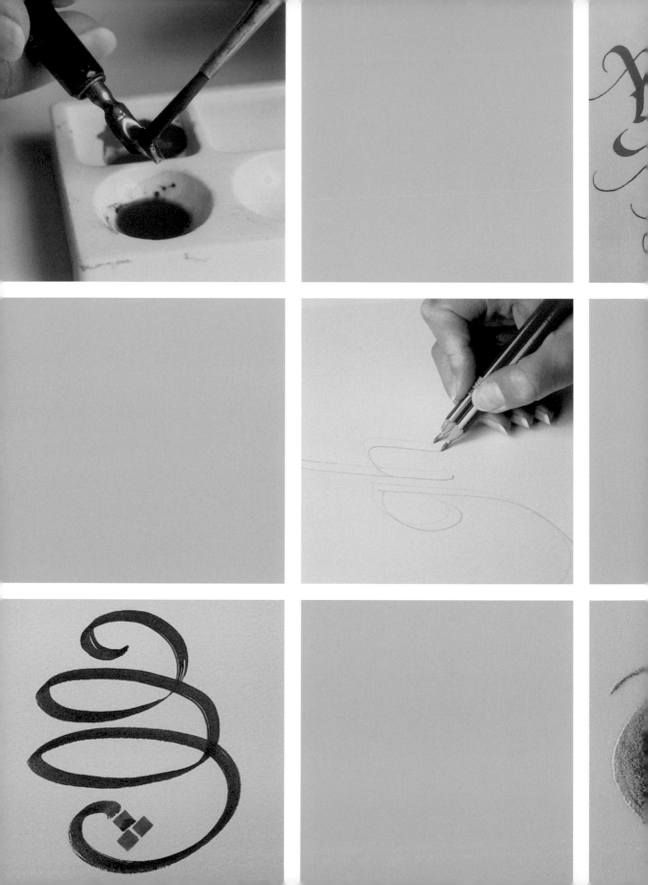

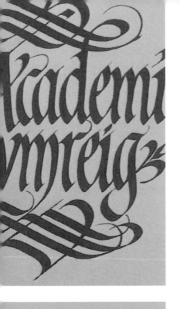

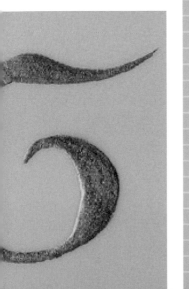

DECORATION

Using Color

The introduction of color into a calligraphic work instantly adds substance and gives another dimension to the piece. In past centuries, as now, the use of color was dictated first by the availability of materials and second by the requirements of the work. Pellucid, uncomplicated color decoration was applied initially to draw attention to specific information and to contrast with the dense blackness of the text.

Color made from rubrica, a red earth, was commonly applied to manuscripts not by the scribes themselves, but by rubricators, who were experts at employing pigment. The "rubric" that they applied might be a number of things, including the title, a heading or an initial letter in the manuscript, notes of instruction in the margin of a text, or an entire paragraph.

The opportunities for including color to some degree paralleled the development of the scripts that they both accompanied and utilized. The versal letter, for example, which was heavily ornamented, blossomed on the pages of broad-pen scripts, creating immediate interest and contrast.

The range of color applications remains largely unchanged since the time of considered and glorious ornamentation of illuminated manuscripts. Color can be included as an entire pictorial piece, as a single capital letter at the beginning of the text, or as individual letters throughout the work.

There is an extensive range of materials that can be used to supply color for the calligrapher. The two most useful sources of color to be laid down for finished work are colored inks and paints. Some consideration needs to be given to selecting the right medium for the work. The medium must be suitable for application with the intended writing instrument, giving sharp edges and hairline serifs or decoration, as required. You must also consider the permanence of the work. Inks with an inherent transparency will have a tendency to fade, unlike opaque designer's colors or gouache.

The paper must also be chosen carefully. If you are using watercolors, for example, it will be necessary to use a paper

USING A LARGE BRUSH

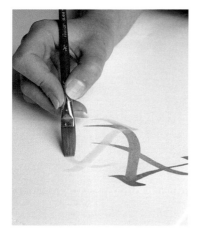 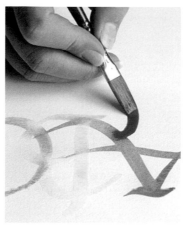 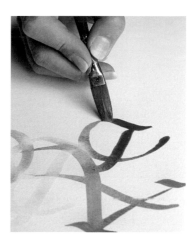

1 Working with color and a large brush is an adventure, and one from which much can be learned. The freedom of movement afforded by the brush, combined with the search for an interesting layout and arrangement of color, is also good for developing personal concepts for use in later works.

2 Placing a second color over a first, while the latter is still wet, can produce exciting results.

3 Occasionally, this wet-into-wet technique results in a muddy mess; but the enjoyment experienced and the discoveries made through your experiments are, initially, more important than achieving a perfect result every time.

Experience will tell you just how much time to allow between applications of color to achieve a more controlled result.

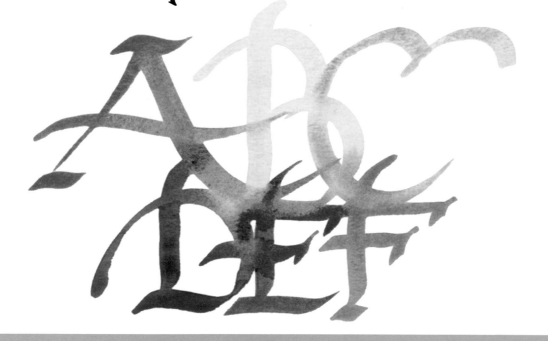

that can absorb the added moisture without having any detrimental effect.

INKS

For single-color work, a good-quality calligraphy ink can be used. These inks are specially formulated, they are waterproof, and they have good permanence. To sum up, they provide a substantial finish to the calligraphic stroke.

DRAWING INKS

These are available in many brilliant, transparent colors and require no mixing, although they can be mixed with each other. Being ready to use, they are a good choice for practice strokes and roughing out color areas, either in text or in decoration, even though the final work may be executed in another medium.

The fluidity of the inks makes them ideal for this purpose, and they can be used directly with nib, brush, or ruling pen. Concentrated watercolors or dyes are mediums that give a very bold finish and can be used directly from the container or diluted with water.

PAINTS

Watercolor is the medium most frequently employed by calligraphers. Individual preference dictates whether to use paint from a pan, cake, or tube. These colors, which need to be mixed with water to create a workable consistency, readily mix with each other to furnish an extensive palette.

Watercolors can provide a wonderful luminous effect. The principle of watercolor work is that the light comes from the substrate—usually white paper. Layers of color can be applied separately, overlapped, or built up one on another. This must be done carefully with fresh color to benefit fully from the effect of these pigments.

Designers' gouache provides a superior source of solid color, not obtainable with translucent watercolors. The opaque color sits on the substrate and light is reflected from the painted surface, so white or colored paper can be used without fear of losing the vibrancy of the paint hues. Water is used to thin and mix gouache and does little to diminish the brilliance of the colors. Color can be laid thinly as a single layer or be strengthened by painting wet into wet, or color mixes can be made in the palette.

APPLYING COLOR

When working with any color system, always mix more than you think the job will actually require, and keep a note of the colors you use and their proportions in the mixtures. You will need to practice mixing colors to a good working consistency so that the paint flows in a manner that will achieve the intended results.

Do plenty of rough workings and test the substrate for absorbency. Always have a sample of your selected paper or board on hand so that you can test the color, both for consistency and for color match.

PREPARING TO USE PAINT WITH A NIB

The paint is prepared in a palette. Water is carefully added with a brush or eyedropper, so that the paint does not become too thin. It is always advisable to test for consistency and color match on a scrap of paper. Use a brush to transfer a small amount of paint onto the nib.

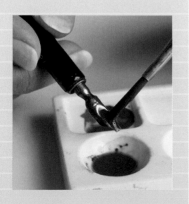

Mix the colors well, check that you have the required color, and keep on checking and stirring so that the colors do not begin to separate out.

There are two agents that you can use to improve paint consistency. The first is gum arabic. Most designers' colors use this as an ingredient. It aids the handling or flow of the paint and slightly increases the gloss of its finish. The other agent is ox gall. Both agents improve the adhesive quality of the paint. When using gum arabic or ox gall, add them to the paint mix very carefully and only one drop

USING A NIB

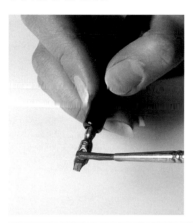

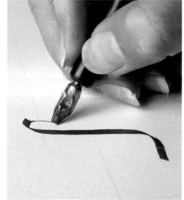

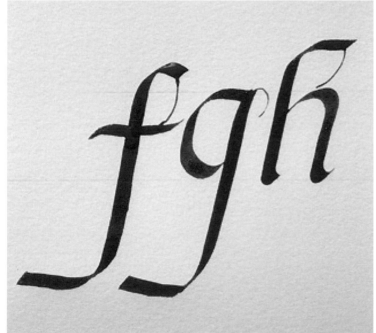

1 Hairline extensions to letters are often easier to form with paint than with ink. Paint takes longer to dry and so enough residue of liquid is available to pull down with the corner of the nib. Load the nib carefully with a brush before starting to work.

2 When executing fine lettering with paint, the nib will require frequent cleaning. This is best done between letters to prevent clogging and to maintain the crisp edge that the lettering style requires.

3 When working with color, care must be taken to maintain an even distribution of color tone, unless an irregularity is being exploited. Hairline extensions are made by lifting the nib and then dragging wet paint with one corner of it. This can be easier to achieve with paint than with other media because paint takes longer to dry. This means that a pool of liquid, which is ready to be pulled into an extension, remains at the beginning or end of the stroke for longer.

The choice of a dark colored paper adds an extra dimension and depth to this work by John Smith. The gouache, with its excellent opacity, sits well on the colored ground. The contrasting colors used for the words by P B Shelley work well together, especially in their arrangement of broken lines. The grouped lines, with color overlapping, add movement to the work, designed to a circular format and transformed visually into a spiral.

at a time. Use a toothpick or matchstick to apply the drops, not a brush.

If you are using a pen, load the nib with a brush, then check that it is not overloaded either by flicking the pen (well away from the final piece), or by writing a small stroke on a scrap sheet. Working with paint, in particular, necessitates cleaning the nib or brush frequently. This should become a habit and should be done even if the tool does not seem to require cleaning.

When the medium is mixed with water, the liquid tends to collect at the bottom of the letter strokes. This may be the intention and can be exploited to the advantage of the work. If, however, this is not what is required, you will need to lower the angle of your work surface toward the horizontal.

Understatement, deliberately limiting the amount of color, can result in a superior finished work. Color that is intended to provide contrast and to draw attention to the work must also supplement it. But if the lettering is not well executed, the use of color will not save the work.

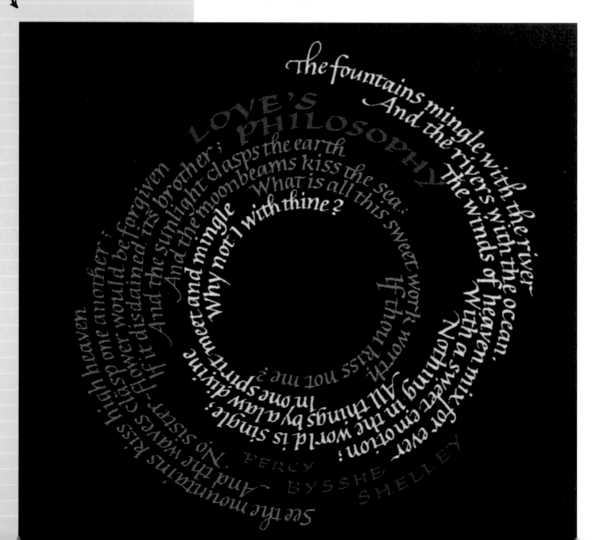

PREPARING A COLORED GROUND

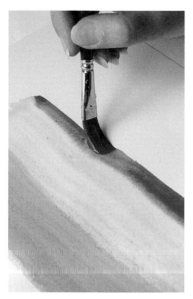

1 Although most calligraphy is done on white or cream paper, a colored ground can often add an extra dimension to a work. To create a delicate wash of color, use thinly diluted watercolor paint applied to pre-dampened paper with a broad flat brush. Color washing works best on heavy or absorbent papers. Be sure to mix plenty of paint so that you don't run out halfway through, and apply the wash quickly to avoid streaks and runs.

2 Allowing different drying times between the application of adjacent colors will permit some of the colors to merge into each other. In well-planned and more complicated works, this can add background interest and suggest visual ideas that can be exploited.

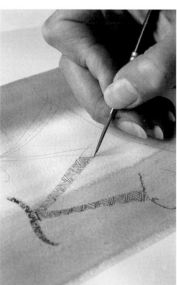

3 Make sure that the paint is absolutely dry before attempting to write on the sheet.

Flourishing

This requires some study before it can be used effectively. Flourishing is the ornamental embellishment of a letter or letters, and there are innumerable examples that you can refer to—in books, manuscripts held in museum collections, and the work of engravers on glass or metal. In all these examples, a wealth of challenging ideas can be confronted. Look for common elements and develop a personal working language for flourishing.

Practice making traditional flourishing shapes and simple marks before attempting to apply the lines as letter extensions.

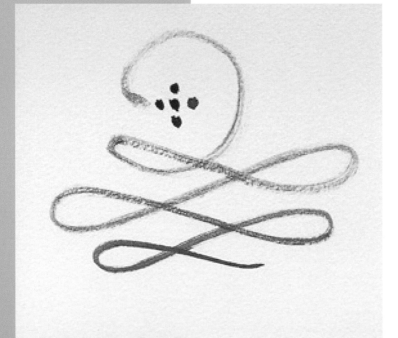

M ake sketches and, where possible, put tracing paper over the flourishing and trace the flowing lines involved. Discover the shape that is formed by the flourishing, what space it occupies, how thick lines cross thin lines and diagonals run parallel.

The most obvious context for flourishing would seem to be as an extension of formal scripts, but this is not its only place. There are plenty of opportunities, but proceed with caution. When learning to apply flourishing, bear in mind that the basic letters of the work must be well formed.

In work that could technically form the basis for splendid flourishing, the nature of the words, or of the job itself, may dictate otherwise. Studying the text together with the guidelines of the brief will quickly reveal whether the work should be treated to a subtle or elaborate amount of flourishing—if any at all. There are occasions when a measure of controlled flourishing is quite sufficient and the result is all the more effective for the restraint with which it is applied.

USING A POINTED BRUSH

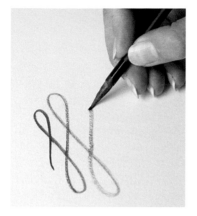

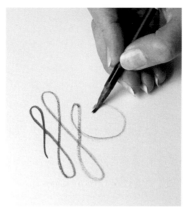

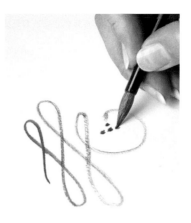

1 Successful flourishing requires practice so that the strokes can be created in a relaxed manner and flow naturally. Flourishes should blend with the work and not appear to be contrived. A pointed brush is an excellent tool to assist in developing a rhythmic and fluid style.

2 The brush moves with great agility to create expressive arcs and lines. Varying the pressure on the brush produces lines that vary from thick to thin in one continuous stroke.

3 Flourishing exercises can be interesting pieces in their own right. Here the addition of red dots made with the tip of the brush, provides a finishing touch.

Other situations provide a challenge that should be met with flourishing that is innovative and inventive.

Begin with simple solutions, always remembering that the strokes must be perceived as a natural extension of the letters, not as additions. They should flow freely and be naturally incorporated into the whole design. They should not bump into, or obscure, the letters of the text. Always plan flourishing well in plenty of rough workings.

Practice with a relaxed arm movement, using whatever instrument feels most comfortable. A fine pointed nib works well. Experiment with taking thin strokes upward and then working the downstrokes by applying more pressure. Applying pressure on upward strokes can be disastrous— the nib digs into the paper and ink splatters on the work.

Accomplished and elaborate flourishing can look wonderful, but it needs a lot of study and practice. As you gain confidence, flourishing will become quite a logical extension to much of your calligraphic work. Sign writing, memorial inscriptions, civic documents, certificates, letterheads, single-letter logos, and delicate personal messages all provide much potential for flourishing.

USING A SQUARE-CUT BRUSH

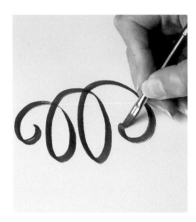 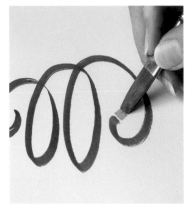 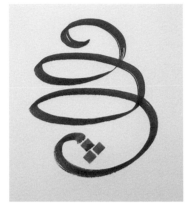 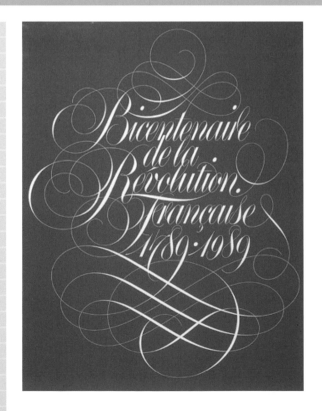

1 A small square-cut brush will mimic the thin and thick lines of a broad nib, but not create too much resistance in its movement.

2 A large square-cut brush is used here to add red dots as a finishing touch.

3 Exercises such as these demonstrate how thick and thin strokes evolve, especially when using a square-cut brush. They also help develop your ideas on layout.

An exuberant display of flourishing using copperplate-style lettering in French by Jean Larcher. The final piece was produced by silkscreening one color in reverse. The artwork was prepared in black on scratchboard.

USING DOUBLE POINTS

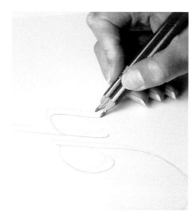

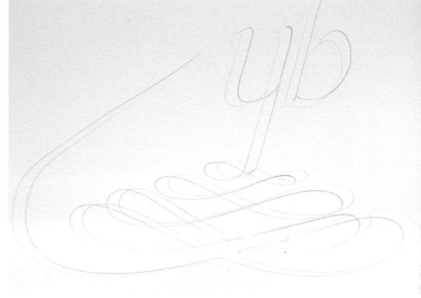

1 Employing double points to make flourishes provides an opportunity to introduce letters to the exercise. The double points are treated in the same manner as a square nib, but can be manipulated with greater freedom of movement across the page.

2 Double pencils allow an energetic flourish to emerge and be applied as an extension to a letter. The flourish here is drawn to resemble a ribbon unfurling.

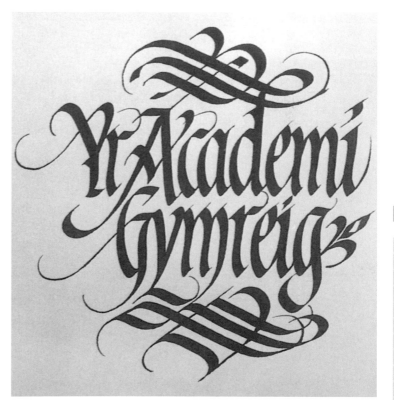

An energetic but controlled flourish in Welsh by Ieuan Rees that adds great interest and balances the work. Note how the bold lines that form the basis of the flourishing are parallel.

Raised Gold

Among the finest medieval manuscripts are those that include the application of gold. Elegant capital letters and complex patterns adorn the pages elevating the manuscript as an item to be admired. To produce such fine work, lengthy processes of preparation were assiduously followed. First, the preparation of the substrate, then the selection and treatment of pigments for color decoration, and, finally, the ground for the gold leaf.

The processes for applying raised gold remain largely unchanged since medieval times. The work is planned and the text written out, leaving the gilding until last. The gold is laid on a prepared ground and, when dry, is brought to a high luster by burnishing.

Raised gold is a particularly fine effect of gilding, as the leaf is laid on a raised ground forming a low "cushion," a three-dimensional element that causes the gold leaf to reflect

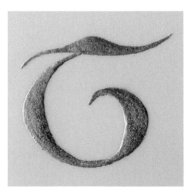

even more brilliance than when it is laid flatly. It catches all the available light that falls on the page as it is viewed and turned.

Gesso provides the ideal ground for raised gold decoration. This is, basically, a mixture of plaster and glue that can be applied with a quill or brush. It has a slightly tacky surface that receives the gold leaf evenly. When dry, it is solid but relatively flexible, so that it will not crack when a page is handled. Preparation of the gesso ground is the most lengthy procedure involved in applying raised gold decoration.

Gold leaf is sold in booklets in which the fine gold is interleaved with tissue. Other metallic leafs are available: palladium, derived from platinum, and silver. The burnisher used to bring up the shine on the gold after it is dry is traditionally made of agate or haematite.

APPLYING RAISED GOLD

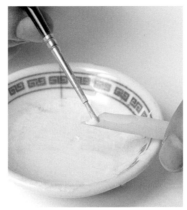

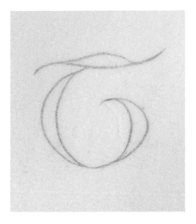

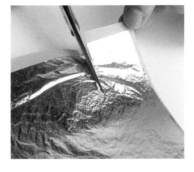

1 Prepare the gesso by breaking up the colored plaster into an egg cup or a small dish. (The plaster is colored so that, when applied to the page, it will show up against the background.) Add a few drops of glair—a solution of water to make the gesso into a workable medium. Leave the mixture to dissolve for at least 20 minutes.

2 Cover the gesso with distilled water and mix to a smooth, creamy consistency. The end of a quill pen, or a bone folder, can be used to stir the solution and get rid of any air bubbles. If bubbles persist, a drop of oil of cloves dripped from the end of a toothpick should solve the problem. The gesso is now ready to be used with a quill or metal nib.

3 The best substrate for working on is vellum. Care must be taken to ensure that the vellum is free of all impurities, such as grease or tackiness. To do this, treat the surface with pumice, and then carefully brush off all the powder.

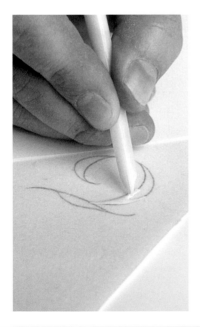

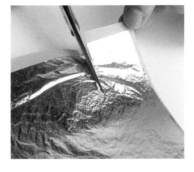

4 Lay the vellum flat on a sheet of glass. Flood the letter with gesso to give a raised "cushion" effect. When the letter is completely filled in with gesso, allow a minimum of 12 hours for it to dry. The drying letter can be left overnight, and the gold applied next day. Sometimes the final result is better for the waiting. Laying the gold must be done quickly, so it is important to have all the necessary materials and equipment on hand before you begin.

5 Gold leaf is a very fine material, so take extra care in its handling. The scissors used to cut the leaf should be cleaned with silk, to stop the material from sticking. The gold leaf is supplied in book form interleaved with tissue paper. Cut through both layers to a size slightly larger than the letterform.

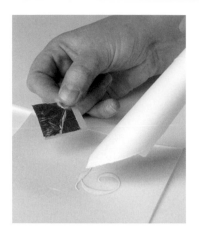

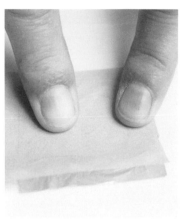

6 Holding the gold leaf with its backing sheet ready, blow gently through a paper cylinder onto the gessoed letter. The still-tacky gesso is now ready to receive the gold. This must be done quickly.

7 Apply firm pressure through the backing sheet, to encourage the gold leaf to adhere to the gesso. Remove the tissue backing sheet, and replace with a piece of crystal parchment.

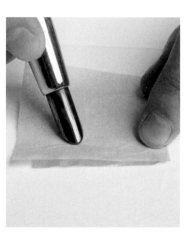

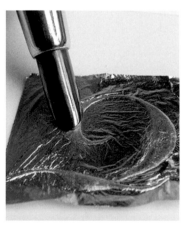

8 Using a haematite or agate burnisher, rub firmly on the crystal parchment. After working with the burnisher, remove the parchment.

9 Clean the burnisher on a piece of silk, and burnish the gold leaf directly. Work the gold leaf around the raised letter, paying particular attention to pressing the gold into and around the edges.

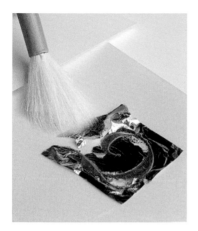

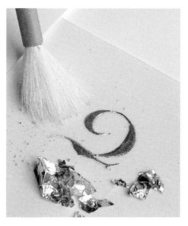

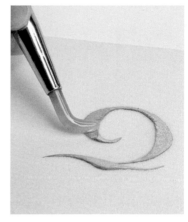

10 Using a dry soft-haired brush, remove the excess gold leaf from around the letter. Use light, short brushstrokes to flick the gold away, rather than dragging the brush.

11 Continue light brushing until all the gold leaf surrounding the gilded letter is removed. A second layer of double gold leaf is now placed over the gilded letter. Crystal parchment is again placed over the gold and firm pressure is applied. Clean off the excess gold with a soft brush as before.

12 Here, a dogtooth agate burnisher is used to work the gold leaf to a final brilliance and smoothness. This burnisher is specially shaped to ensure that the leaf is worked into the edges and rounded parts of the letter.

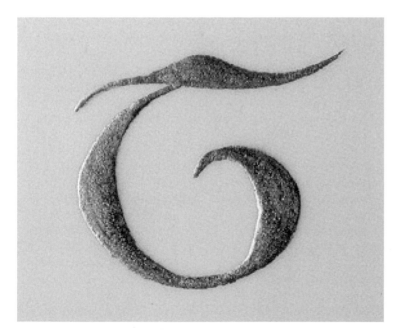

13 The gold leaf is now burnished until it is completely smooth and shines brightly when it catches the light.

Gilding

There are two distinct techniques for applying gold decoration to calligraphic design. One is the flat method of gilding, the other raised gold. The true art of illumination stemmed from the practice of applying a medium with a metallic finish that would reflect any surrounding light, although the term also referred to the introduction of any color in order to draw attention to something in the text.

Many of the finest manuscripts of the past two thousand years are richly adorned with gold. In Greece, where the concept of working with gold may have arrived from Asia or from Egypt, there were early references to some of the scribes as "writers in gold." There is evidence to suggest that, by the second century AD, Rome was influenced by the Greek example. Gloriously ornate manuscripts were produced solely for the wealthy citizens. For most people, the exorbitant cost of materials, particularly gold and vellum, prohibited their use. To make vellum, early scribes meticulously prepared the skins of calf, kid, or lamb, if necessary staining them to the color required for the baseground of the manuscript. Sometimes the entire skin would be gilded. This involved many processes including, after the initial washing, beating, stretching, and drying, smearing with egg whites, and then more washing, drying, rubbing, pressing, polishing, and finally applying gold leaf. Egg whites were usually used as the fixative for the application of the gold.

The many ancient recipes for preparing to work with gold read like an alchemy instruction book, the only difference being that the scribes already had the precious metal. Other metals were also used, including silver, brass, and copper. If none of these was available, a scribe could simulate gilding using tin and saffron.

Great care is required in the application of gold, as it remains an expensive commodity. Gold leaf, or sheets of gold transfer leaf, is excellent for decorating a page with a highlighted initial letter, filling in an ornament, or providing a baseground. The leaf must be laid on an adhesive ground. The process of laying

USING THE FLAT GILDING METHOD

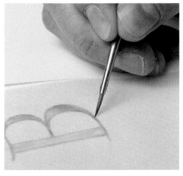

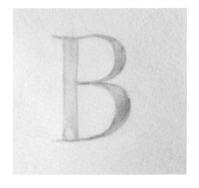

1 One of the most accessible methods of applying gold to a work is the modern flat method. Begin by preparing all the equipment and materials. Then make a very light pencil outline of the letter to which the gold is to be applied.

2 Gum ammoniac is traditionally used as size. PVA, a plastic adhesive, also works well, although it is less long-lasting. Mix the size with a little gouache and water, if needed. The color provided by the gouache makes the letter visible. Paint the outline and fill in the letter with the mixture using a small pointed brush.

3 Allow the letter to dry completely. Depending on the working conditions, this can take from 30 minutes to one hour.

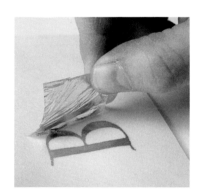

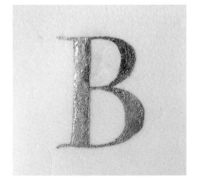

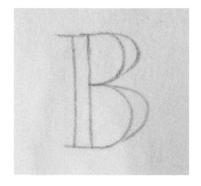

4 Carefully cut out a piece of gold leaf large enough to cover the letter completely. Breathe on the letter to create a tacky, adhesive surface ready to receive the gold leaf. Press the gold down firmly with the thumb, working gently over the area being gilded. Apply a second layer of gold in a similar manner if required.

5 Brush away the excess gold leaf with a soft, long-haired Chinese brush. Burnish the letter with great care, using a burnisher made from agate or haematite.

6 The use of PVA will not give the superior quality of finish obtained with raised gold. However, the method provides a more readily accessible way of applying gold and can produce pleasing results.

gold leaf is very delicate, as it is a fine, clinging material.

The less lustrous powder gold is obtainable either loose or in cake form. When mixed with distilled water to a working consistency, it creates a reasonable finish. Gum arabic used as a binder improves its adherence to the page. Powder gold can be applied with a quill pen, nib, or brush, and is a direct and less complicated medium for gilding than gold leaf. Both types of gold can be burnished when absolutely dry, but powder gold never attains the gleaming surface quality of burnished gold leaf.

Inexpensive alternatives to real gold are naturally inferior in quality, especially in the finish. Various metallic gouaches, inks, and fiber-tip pens are available. These are all excellent for use in rough workings and may, in some circumstances, be suitable for finished work.

PREPARATION FOR GILDING

There are two materials that can be used as the size to prepare the surface of a page for gilding. One is polyvinyl acetate (PVA), a plastic adhesive. It consists of resin in suspension in water, together with plasticizers and stabilizers that prevent settling out of the resin. When PVA is applied to a surface, the water evaporates and the resin particles coalesce into a continuous film.

The other type of size, gum ammoniac, requires preparation. Supplied in solid form, it must

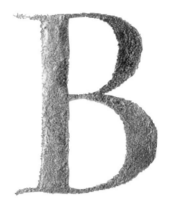

first be reduced to fine granules and soaked overnight in distilled water. Next, stir the gum and strain it through a fine mesh of muslin or nylon. Gently heat the strained mixture and strain again. The straining process may have to be repeated several times until the resulting liquid is of a suitable consistency for use with a pen. Any gum not used can be stored in an airtight container.

Before applying either type of size, color it slightly with some gouache so that you will be able to see it clearly on the page. Check that the work surface is level, so that the size will not collect at the bottom of a letter stem or decoration. You can apply size with a pen or brush.

An extravagant use of gilding is displayed on this page from the **Codex Aureus**. An interesting balance has been achieved in applying the gold alternately to a line of letters, and as a background to the next line. Traditional elements of ornament decorate the page.

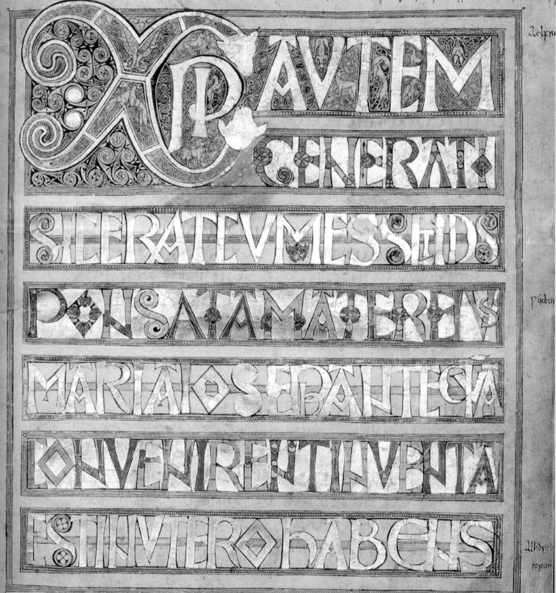

Illumination

Initially, illumination referred to the addition of color (red lead) to a first letter or word to indicate a change in the text (written in black). Some minimal color decoration may also have been used. In time, the interpretation of illumination expanded to include manuscripts on stained vellum adorned with letters and decoration executed in gold and silver. These precious metals reflected light.

Initially, the scribe responsible for writing the text added ornamentation but, in time, as different aspects of the work developed, other craftspeople joined the workshops. The illuminator, as the most skilled person, became designer, colorist, and illustrator and, with great style, accomplished the task of bringing life to the page.

Illumination is really about the calligrapher's own experience, especially in terms of design sensibility and color sensitivity. It presents a wonderful opportunity to exploit pattern, from the most simple to the outrageous, as well as color, texture, and pictorial imagery.

Decorated letters enhance calligraphy. These are some traditional arrangements.

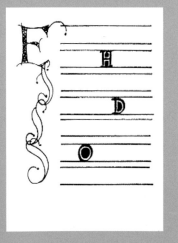

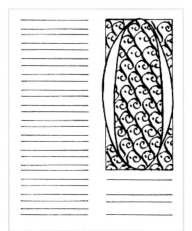

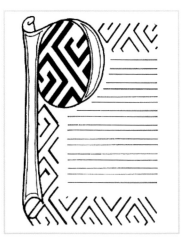

STUDYING ILLUMINATION

Excellent examples of illumination can be found in museums, libraries, art collections, and books. To begin to appreciate the intricate nature of these works, make sketches and notes of solutions that appeal. Looking at the works can be an overwhelming experience, so start by studying one section at a time.

For example, select an enlarged letter and identify its origins—perhaps Roman, Uncial, or Versal. Is the letter distorted or elongated? Are areas of the letter decorated? Does the decoration extend to counter spaces inside or outside the letter? Do the strokes or stem of the letter have applied decoration? How has the scribe treated the serif?

Work through the ways in which each of these areas has been manipulated. Find where patterning is repeated, or identical motifs are used, sometimes with simple variations. Follow foliage or knotwork patterns; what shaped spaces do they occupy? Circular? Triangular?

Breaking down a complex design into understandable sections helps to demystify the art of illumination. The same procedure can be extended to borders, margin decoration, and the whole relationship of the illumination to the text. At the same time, you can study the quality of the color work and gilding to see which techniques might be appropriate for your own illuminations.

Lots of rough workings and color experimentation are the cornerstones of good illumination. This is an opportunity for great freedom of expression in calligraphic design. Build a checklist of design considerations so you can refer to the options. Basic ingredients are dot, line, shape, and color. Many patterns can be built based solely on dots or circles. Treatment for an initial letter may include enlargement, elongation, creating a picture that incorporates the letter, applying texture to the body of the letter, or letters made out of patterns, leaves, or animals; use similar ideas for counter spaces and borders.

When working out the area to accommodate the illumination, do not ignore the text area. Indicate text with lines in your rough workings and aim toward a balanced look for the final work.

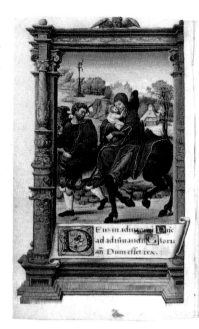

This spread from an early sixteenth-century French Book of Hours has an uncomplicated layout. A decorative border frames the Humanistic script inscribed text, which has illuminated initial letters.

Ornament

Changes in artistic style can often be seen as running parallel to social and political changes occurring in particular places and times. The evolution of ornament falls within this pattern of events, reflecting the rise and decline of early civilizations and the interchange of ideas between different cultures brought about by trade, military conquest, and religious influences.

An example of this was the development of decorative patterning derived from Islamic silk fabrics. Following ancient tradition, the silk weavers incorporated goodwill expressions in their designs. With the increase of trade around the Mediterranean, the art of silk weaving spread and these Muslim fabrics were copied, including the inscriptions. As the words were incomprehensible to European weavers, scripts were copied as mere scribbles. Gradually, however, some of the Arabic letters were put into more symmetrical forms for mechanical weaving, resulting in "mock Arabic" devices.

The Romans, more concerned with expanding their boundaries and creating wealth than with developing an artistic identity, initially took their influences from Etruria and Greece. As their wealth and power increased, they employed Greek teachers and, in time, established their own recognizable monumental works. Roman ornamental style subsequently overpowered that of the Greek masters. The Romans used ornament in a naturalistic manner, as shown in their architecture; decorated capitals with curling leaves, entablatures with ox heads and lions, rosettes, and festoons were all incorporated.

The collapse of the Roman Empire heralded a linking of Christian ideals and the remains of classical art. With strong Byzantine influence, ornamental art underwent a transformation. By the fifth century, the symbol of the cross was included in many inscriptions, providing a base for allover patterns and the development of the "gammadion" device. The greatest exponents of ornament were the scribes of Ireland, responsible for the fine Celtic tradition.

Succeeding centuries saw a flourishing of key patterns, intricate knotwork, spirals, mosaic, and geometric patterning. Elements from the natural world were drawn on, including vegetation—both imagined and real—leaves, flowers, palm fronds, lotus, acanthus, and vine. Animals were an important feature, making a major contribution to ornament design—dogs, lions, lambs, snakes, eagles, doves, peacocks, fish, and fantastic imaginary beasts. In medieval and Renaissance manuscripts, miniature paintings and detailed figurative illustrations incorporated within the letters reflected the life of the time.

DESIGNING ORNAMENT

Ornament may fill an entire margin, or create a border for the text or a background for a capital letter. Delicate patterns and repeated symbols can complete a line where the text falls short and does not align. The intention in using ornament in calligraphic design is to achieve absolute harmony throughout the entire work, and so it must be planned in from the start, not added as an afterthought.

Special attention needs to be paid to proportion and the symmetry of shapes and colors. Begin by including simple geometric figures that constitute the basic vocabulary of ornament: square, circle, triangle, oval, and lozenge. Introduce a connecting element with lines, chains, spiraling

BASIC METHODS OF ARRANGEMENT

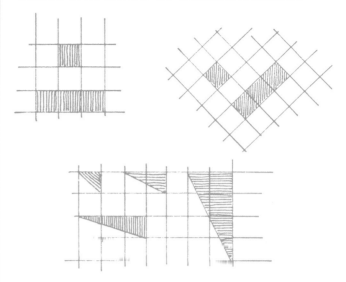

1 The best starting point for learning to apply ornament is to study basic construction methods. Simple patterns can be generated on a network of lines crossing each other at different angles. Begin by building patterns along lines placed at right angles to one another and at equal distances (squared paper is useful here). Fill in individual shapes to produce squares and diamonds, and adjacent squares to produce oblongs. Introduce oblique lines that cut across the squares and oblongs to produce triangles.

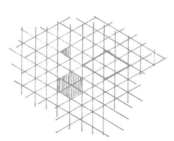

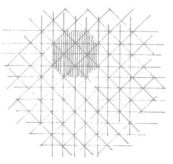

2 To create ornament based on hexagonal shapes, the lines are placed at an angle of 30°, and crossed by vertical lines.

3 Placing lines at an angle of 45°, and then crossing them with vertical and horizontal lines, will create octagonal shapes.

THINGS TO CONSIDER

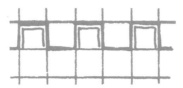

1 Altering the lines and shapes applied to the basic network of lines begins to extend the language of ornament. Here the horizontal and vertical lines provide the framework of a pattern used extensively in heraldry, known as embattled.

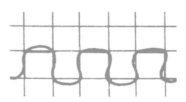

2 Here the lines of the embattled pattern have been curved in order to create a meander.

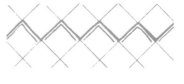

3 A squared grid, set at 45° to the horizontal, creates the diamond, which is used here as a framework for the chevron zigzag.

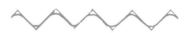

4 Curving the apexes of the zigzag in this network creates a wave.

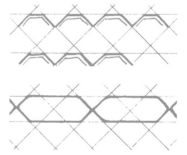

5 The same network, with the addition of horizontal lines, becomes the basis for the blunted zigzag and the interlaced patterns.

cables, interlacings, zigzags, waves, or a running scroll. Repetition of any of these motifs can create pattern areas within the design. More ambitious solutions can be attempted by starting with basic shapes and then including simple motifs from the natural world.

Consider carefully, through rough working sketches, the power of a simple design solution, incorporating selective ornament with an elegant letter. Compare this with a fussy and over-embellished design where the strength of the letter shape is diminished.

The size of ornament should relate closely to the scale of writing and size of the page. If the ornament is in a manuscript

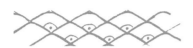

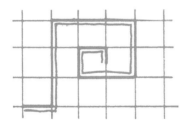

6 The geometric lines of the zigzag are here rounded to produce the scallop. The interlaced pattern is adapted to produce the scale pattern.

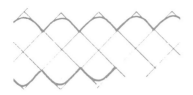

7 The squared network provides the foundation for construction of the fret. This familiar geometrical figure forms the basis of many fine ornamental borders.

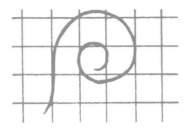

8 The spiral is created by rounding the straight lines and sharp angles of the fret.

9 The wave and the running scroll are adaptations of the spiral.

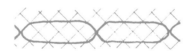

10 The interlacing constructed on the network of crossed diagonal lines can be enlarged to form a double wave or meander.

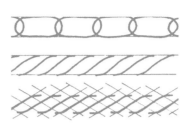

11 By converting the rectilinear network to one of circles and ellipses, further ornamental elements can be added to your repertoire. These include the chain and cable.

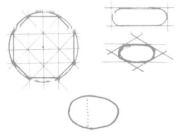

12 The curved series evolves from a softening of the basic shapes The octagon becomes a circle. The oblong and some proportions of the diamond are altered into elliptical shapes. The ellipse and the circle produce the oval.

book, the scale should remain consistent throughout the volume. Take care in selecting the ingredients of ornament drawn from the natural world—use a good model. If the ornament is imagined and repeated, be consistent in the repeats: work from a well-prepared finished rough. Spirals, knotwork, frets, and other linear forms require careful attention. The construction methods of Celtic ornament provide the best key to this kind of interlacing. To avoid confusion, complete each stage of the construction throughout the entire design before moving on to the next stage.

LAYING OUT ORNAMENT

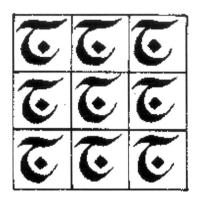

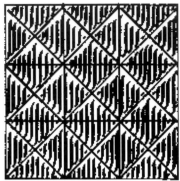

1 The diagrams on the previous page illustrate some of the elemental forms and lines found in styles of ornamental art, and upon which more elaborate details can be built. The same principle of networks is used to show some of the methods of laying out ornament. The method shown here involves filling in each square, in a technique known as diapering.

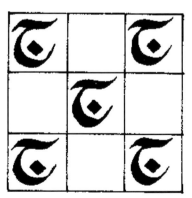

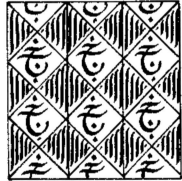

2 Working on the same squared grid, but omitting alternate squares. This method is known as checkering.

3 Diapering and checkering can be effectively combined to create solid patterns.

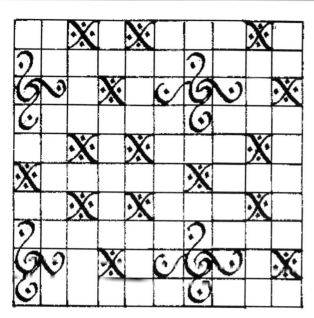

4
Employing the same principle, but allowing larger spaces between the filled-in areas. This is referred to as spotting or powdering.

5
Applying the ornament in rows, and leaving some rows void, is known as striping. Versions of striping constructed in a narrower vein are called banding.

6
A combination of striping and banding produces another layout, which is called paneling.

COMBINING ORNAMENT AND LETTERS

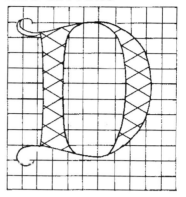

1
Working with these methods of organizing ornament provides a valuable foundation for illumination and decoration. In this example, the basic squared grid is drawn, and the letter is superimposed. The letter has a network of lines arranged at 30° to the horizontal.

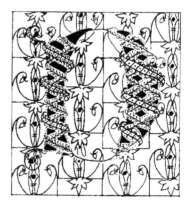

2
Using the arrangements of lines, ornament is applied to both the letter and the base ground. The squared grid provides the basis for a repeat pattern. To repeat this particular pattern, the lateral repetition has been achieved by lowering the pattern to fit two sections together.

GEOMETRIC DESIGN

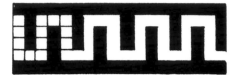

1 Fret patterns can be used as borders on their own, or they can be incorporated with ornament, and embrace an enlarged letter. The basic structure of fret patterns can be used as a framework for decoration not composed solely of straight lines. The simplest forms use lines that are all either vertical or horizontal. The distance between the lines is the same as the width of the lines. As with other basic ornament structures, using squared paper will help you to plan your designs accurately. This geometric border is six widths wide, the top and bottom lines are continuous, and the vertical lines are three widths high. Developing this nature of analysis is the best method of understanding how to construct these designs.

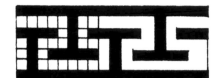

2 This pattern is seven widths wide. It is an expanded version of the first example, with the introduction of horizontal lines. In these patterns, the "negative" shapes formed by the ground (in this case, the white of the paper) are as important to the appearance of the finished design as the "positive" shapes of the marks made.

3 The pattern below is of interlacing strap work. To build patterns in this style, begin working with vertical and horizontal lines, and lines placed at a 45° angle. This particular example has been expanded and used at a flatter angle.

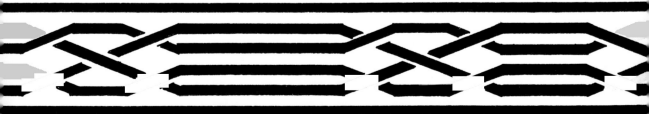

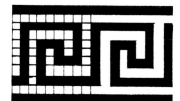

4 This pattern is known as the key pattern. It shows a balance of black and white (negative and positive), which is an important feature in fret designs.

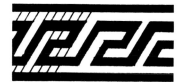

5 The introduction of slanting lines to the framework produces a sloping fret. Here the horizontal lines are retained, but the vertical lines are replaced by lines set at an inclined angle.

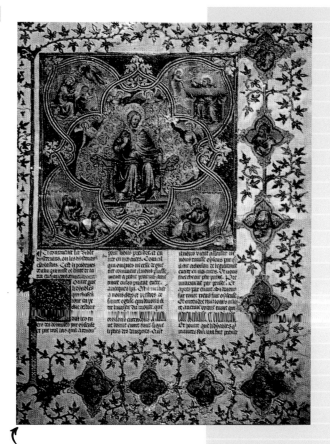

In the wide margins of this page from the fourteenth-century *Bible Historiale*, decorated "barbed" quatrefoils containing individual portraits set against patterned backgrounds are placed at evenly spaced intervals. The vine provides a linking device, and anchors the pictures to the page.

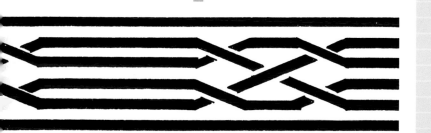

Illustration

When combining illustration with calligraphy, it is important to create harmony between both elements. The illustration should reflect the square-edged pen, as do many early manuscripts, with line drawings making full use of the implement to produce varied stroke widths. Textures can be built up by cross-hatching or by moving the pen angle from a thin stroke gradually through to a thick stroke position.

There is no easy way to learn how to draw with a square nib and, if you do not regard yourself as an illustrator, the only way to succeed is by involvement and practice. One of the best things you can do is to look at photographic and printed references.

Once you have an idea of what image you want to use to accompany a piece of calligraphy, search through your own books, photographs, and pamphlets, or through those in your local library, for suitable images. Searching for material will heighten your awareness of the images you see every day. A scrapbook of likely subject matter is a wonderful idea and takes very little time to add to each week. References should also be as detailed as possible so that new images can readily and accurately be created from them at any opportunity.

Once the necessary references have been found, you will need to transfer them to tracing paper. If the size of the illustration required is the same as that of the reference material, it can be traced directly onto the tracing paper, using a hard pencil (or lead in a technical pencil). Take care to interpret the image exactly, because what is produced on the tracing sheet will be the image traced down on the finished piece of work. Once the tracing is completed, the sheet must be turned over and the underside of the drawing area shaded over with a softer pencil. Turn the tracing paper over again so that the image side faces upward and position it on the finished surface of the work, using masking tape at the head (top) to hold it gently in place. Then trace the drawing down by going over the lines of the image using a hard, sharp pencil. When completed, lift the tracing sheet, without unfastening, to make sure that the drawing has

ILLUSTRATION 105

TRACING TECHNIQUES

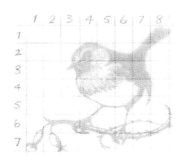

1 Confine the illustration to a gridded square on tracing paper.

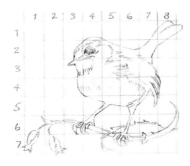

2 Draw a gridded square to the required enlargement and plot the image on the grid.

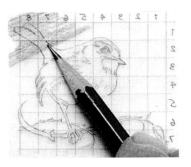

3 Shade over the underside of the tracing.

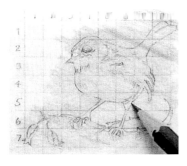

4 Trace the image onto the finished surface.

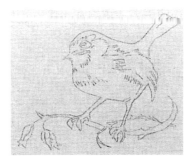

5 The traced image on the finished surface.

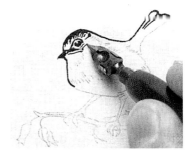

6 Ink in the initial outline and build up the illustration.

been successfully transferred to the finished surface. The faint image must now be inked in with a fine, square-ended nib. Build up the image slowly, referring to the original reference for the finer points.

Should the reference material found not be the correct size for the design, it will be necessary either to enlarge or to reduce the image. First contain the illustration within a square or rectangle on a sheet of tracing paper, subdividing this by small grid squares. The size required should then be drawn as a square or rectangle on another sheet and subdivided as before. Number the squares horizontally and vertically on both sheets of paper and plot your image from the reference material to the correctly sized grid.

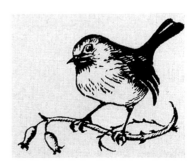

Borders

Borders define a space and can "tidy up" a piece of visual work, but cannot save it if the letterforms and spacing are not well planned in the first place. To demonstrate the power of the border, take a freely drawn piece of lettering or ornament and simply surround it with straight lines. The difference in visual impact is immediate; the effect is the same as framing a picture.

JOINTS FOR BORDERS

The structure of a border framing a work needs consideration. Frames are formed in several ways, including oblique, square, and joggled miter. The corner is the best place to start when designing a border to form a full or semi-enclosure.

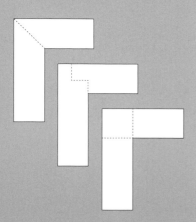

Borders can be incorporated very successfully in many designs. Surrounded totally or in part by a border, a block of text or lines of information on a card can be greatly enhanced. Verses of a poem can be separated by a single line of patterning. Borders should complement the calligraphy; they should not overpower the text, nor look too timid. Too much elaboration can easily detract from the overall appeal of the work.

There are four basic components of border design: repeat horizontal marks, or filling-in worked as a continuous running pattern; a series of vertical marks; a fusion of horizontal and vertical elements; and an arrangement of panels. Put more succinctly, the simplest options are spot, horizontal, vertical, and oblique marks.

Borders should be related to the nature of the work. This is more obvious in other craft areas, but should not be ignored in calligraphy. You can render the writing without embellishment and, without any loss of meaning or intent, surround it with a highly decorative and well-constructed border that also gives great visual and aesthetic impact.

It takes careful consideration and artistic judgment to achieve the correct proportions of a border and its overall value in the work. There is no reason for a border to be straight or for the boundaries to be parallel. It can surround an irregular space and have straight lines on the outer perimeter.

The corners of borders need careful planning, too. When you have made a clear decision as to the nature of the join, whether it is to be oblique, square, or joggled miter, the object is then to design with the join, and this does not necessarily mean either to accentuate it or to conceal it.

FIBER-TIP BORDER

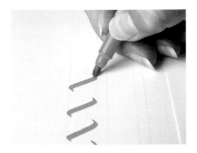 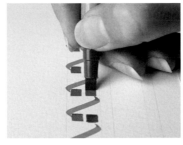 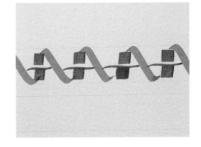

1 Fiber-tip pens with chiseled nibs are useful for working out border patterns, being instant in use and available in a variety of colors. Employing basic broad pen strokes, a line is worked through to the end.

2 Turning a thick pen to an angle of 90° to the horizontal writing line, square dots are placed at the top and base of the slanted line. Then the same pen, held at about 10° to the horizontal, is used to produce a thin, graceful stroke.

3 This red and green border could have more lines and shapes added, or, as here, be regarded as complete.

Sources of ideas for borders abound; start building a border repertoire. For example, make a study of brick bonds, embroidery, or wrought- and cast-iron objects. Such items provide a wealth of line qualities, shapes, and patterns. Make sketches with a pencil, then put tracing paper over your sketch and, using a nib, go over the drawing in ink, selecting simple repeated components. Use these to create an original border.

TOOLS AND TECHNIQUES

Mix and match techniques in your designs: for example, use broken rules interspersed with dots made with a broad nib. Almost any tool is suitable for building up a border—brush, pen, fiber-tip pen, or pencil. Introducing color to a border

requires some planning but, used well, it can be very effective.

Working on squared paper will help build your confidence, giving a framework to the design as you twist and turn the broad nib to invent new arrangements. This exploration also makes a good practice exercise.

Spend some time roughing out the design of the border, especially on the critical decision as to whether it will form a full or partial enclosure for the text. A semi-enclosure is most likely if a decorative heading is part of the piece. If you are confident that line drawing is one of your strengths, the border might include small concealed images relating to the text.

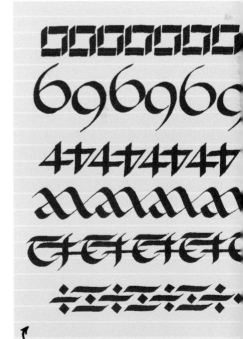

The broad pen can be used to produce simple and pleasing marks that, either alone or in combination, can be repeated to create a decorative border. Changing the pen angle will increase the variety and interest even within the same border.

CARTOUCHES

Although not strictly calligraphic, the cartouche is a device worth considering. Cartouches evolved from an ancient art applied to paper and parchment labels used to hold inscriptions or badges. The edges were cut in an intricate manner that resulted in ornamental curling of the labels, usually into scroll forms. The shapes evolved further in the forms of shields, and eventually panels were cast or carved in order to enclose an inscription, although they were sometimes left blank. In either state, they constituted an important element in design, especially to offset, or to draw attention to, a more engaging ornament.

Calligraphers can refer to old cartouche designs as a rich source of ideas applicable to name cards, heraldic work, quotations, and many other calligraphic works.

BLACK AND WHITE BORDER

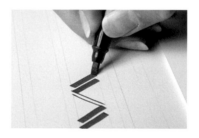

1 The width of stroke varies according to the direction in which the pen is moved, though the nib angle remains fixed.

2 Holding the pen at the same angle used for downward but moving in an upward direction produces thin strokes.

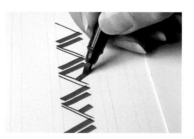

3 A short, thick stroke is inserted between the major lines of the pattern to break up the white space. The lines are first applied along the bottom of the design, before working through the top row.

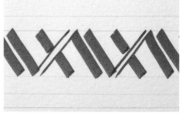

4 The thin and thick strokes form the basic pattern. The application of additional shorter strokes to break up the white space produces a more interesting and pleasing result.

LETTER BORDERS

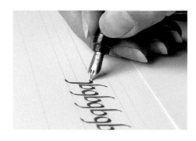

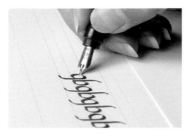

1 Letter shapes can be very effective as a border—especially if the letters are chosen to represent or to allude to something referred to in the piece they surround.

2 Repeating the letters, with their elegant proportions and thick and thin strokes, leads to a perception of an arrangement of shapes rather than letters.

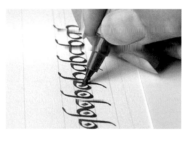

3 The inclusion of a spot color, as a simple device, can add a surprise element and further disguise the actual letter shapes.

BROAD BRUSH BORDERS

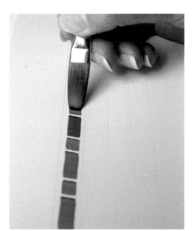

1 A brush with a square-cut end can be used to create a border composed of simple repeated shapes.

2 This example is based on a brick bonding design. The same arrangement can be made using a broad nib.

4 In the finished piece, the letters have become mere vehicles in the creation of this border. The work has a balance of black and white and reads as a row of shapes and lines, rather than letters.

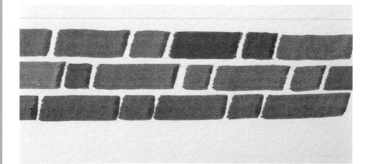

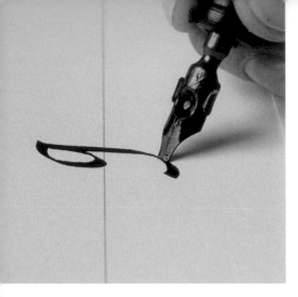

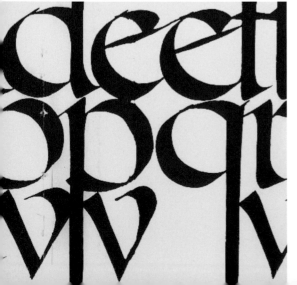

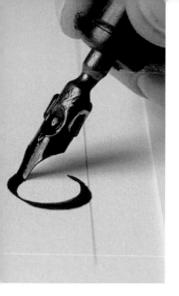

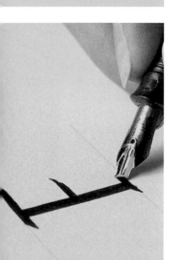

THE ALPHABETS

Roman Alphabets

The great legacy of the Romans includes fine letterforms of splendid proportions and sublime elegance. In keeping with other developments in Roman culture, the letterforms matured over several centuries. The shapes of the letters have a strong connection with the introduction of the rounded arch and vault into architectural style.

UNDERSTANDING THE SYMBOL

Where appropriate, a symbol indicating the suggested nib width, letter height, and pen angle accompanies each alphabet: use this as a guide only. Whatever size nib is used, the height of the letter is always determined using a "ladder" of nib widths.

a refers to the ascender height
c refers to the height of the capital letter
x refers to the x-height—that is, the height of the body of the letter

b refers to the baseline where the body of the lower case letter sits or the base of the capital sits
d refers to where the descender finishes

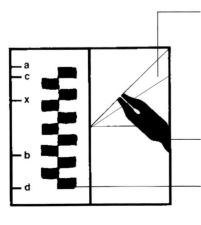

pen angle hold your pen over the nib to ensure that it is at the right angle before you start: when more than one angle line is shown, this indicates there is a range of angles for that hand

nib width the correct width of the pen is shown

ladder to determine letter height

To record an event, Roman capitals were extensively used, incised in stone or marble on monuments, tombs, and arches. Many fine examples of this alphabet, executed by Roman master craftsmen, can still be found. The execution of the letters was not confined to the chisel. Reed brushes and pens and quill pens also produced the perfect proportions and balance of elegant thick and thin strokes.

The Roman square capitals incised in stone were called capitalis. When practiced with a square-cut reed pen or quill, they were known as Quadrata. The Quadrata required exceedingly painstaking execution to achieve the forms correctly. Quite quickly, the rustic forms succeeded the round forms for use in manuscripts. These were letters of a style that could be written at greater speed and with some economy of materials.

A A B B B C C D D D
E E F G H I J K K
L M M N N O O O
P Q R S S T U V V
W W W X Y Z Z

The square capitals continued to be well represented in headings, initial letters, and special applications, as they are to this day.

CLASSICAL ROMAN CAPITALS

The elegant style of classical Roman capitals survives most clearly in the stone-carved inscriptions of imperial architecture and monuments. This alphabet is a modern pen-written version based on those carved forms.

The accompanying diagrams show the order and direction of the pen strokes by which the character is formed: the square-tipped pen is drawn across the paper, never pushed against the grain. The serifs, or finishing strokes, are modeled on the style originally typical of chiseled lettering; they are not natural pen forms, and they require a delicate touch and some dextrous manipulation of the pen.

CONSTRUCTION

The origins of modern letterforms in the western world lie in the classical Roman alphabet of 23 letters. The letters J, U, and W were added during the Middle Ages.

Close study of the letter shapes reveals adherence to basic geometric principles. The letters are carefully constructed using the square and subdivisions of it. The rounded letters C, G, O, and Q can be represented by a circle or part of a circle within the square.

The annotated letters show the order and direction of the strokes forming the classical Roman capitals alphabet. Not all serifs are found naturally with the pen; they have to be manipulated with the top or corner of the nib, as seen in D and K.

The pen angle for this vertical hand varies from 5° for the serifs to 20°–30° for most of the strokes. An angle of 45° is needed for the majority of diagonal strokes. A steeper angle is used for the slanted strokes of M and N, and a flat pen (0°) for the diagonal of Z. The pen moves from the top to the bottom of all vertical and diagonal strokes.

The letter height is 10 nib widths. Meticulous attention must be paid to both the height and width of the letters to achieve and maintain their elegant proportions.

SERIFS

The serifs require further manipulation of the pen, including using only the corner of the nib to complete their fine endings. There are variations in the style and application of serifs, and some are more difficult to execute than others.

The simplest serif is added as a single separate stroke—a hairline formed by turning the pen to the flat angle (0°) for the horizontal stroke.

A bolder serif can be executed as a precursor to or an extension of a stroke.

The classical Roman form has a considered serif extending on both sides of the upright stroke. There is an almost imperceptible flaring of the upright before it comes to rest in the serif. These elegant endings involve much turning of the pen.

Apart from in C, G, and S, all serifs are parallel to the writing line. A concise four-stroke pattern produces the desired effect. The first stroke is the vertical, the second the hairline —in some styles this is slightly concave toward the middle. The third and fourth strokes are identical, but reversed on either side of the vertical, joining the extremes of the hairline serif to the upright with a gentle curve.

This procedure is the same for serifs at the top and bottom of the letters.

ROMAN ALPHABET

Roman letters can be written with a broad pen, held at an angle of 30° for most of the strokes. Diagonal strokes require a steeper pen angle (45°), and the middle stroke of the Z is made with a much flatter angle. The serifs require further manipulation of the pen, including using only the corner of the nib to complete their fine endings.

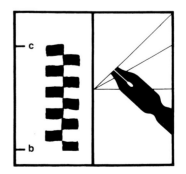

ROMAN LOWER CASE

This alphabet is designed as a complement to the preceding capitals; the flat Roman serifs are seen in k, v, w, x, and y, and at the base of each letter, while the verticals have slanted serifs formed by a slight sideways and upward movement in beginning the stroke, before the pen is pulled smoothly downward. There was no directly comparable contemporary form of what are now called lower-case letters corresponding to the original Roman capitals. The shorter, more rounded forms with ascending and descending strokes were fully evolved in early minuscule scripts, which in turn were readapted by later writing masters and type designers to an overall style and proportion corresponding to the classical squared capitals.

Roman lower-case letters: these Roman minuscule letters are formed directly with the pen. The angle of the pen is 30° except for base serif formation.

a b c
d e f g
h i j
k l m n o p
q r s t u
v w x y z

COMPOUND ROMAN CAPITALS

Delicate proportions and finely varied strokes create a sophisticated modern adaptation of the Roman squared capitals. In this case, the thick and thin stroke variations do not correspond to the actual pen width: the heavier vertical stems and swelling curves are created by outlining the shape and filling in with solid color, in a manner similar to the traditional tendering of decorative Versals. Fine hairlines are used to terminate the individual elements, cutting across the width of the vertical and diagonal strokes with a deliberate yet subtle emphasis. There is no attempt to round out the serifs as in the classical Roman capitals.

Compound Roman capitals: built-up letterforms are almost always in color. The skeleton of the letter is drawn and filled with fluid color. The fine serif is in lieu of the Roman serif.

A B C D
E F G H
I J K L
M N O P Q
R S T U
V W X Y Z

FORMING ROMAN LETTERS

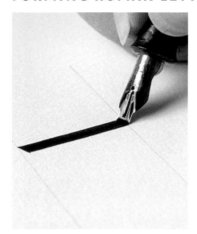

1 Holding the script pen at the correct 30° angle, draw the first downstroke.

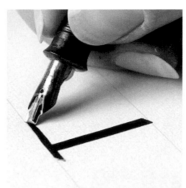

2 The first cross-stroke is then drawn in, which incorporates the correctly angled serif on the left (the correctly held 30° angle of the pen makes the cross-stroke slightly thinner).

3 The second cross-stroke is drawn in, making sure that the pen remains consistently at a 30° angle.

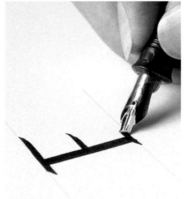

4 The base serif is then added. The height of the completed letter should be exactly 10 nib widths.

MODERN PEN-DRAWN ROMAN LETTERING

This freely worked lower-case alphabet written by the American scribe Arthur Baker employs the unusual elongation of extended strokes, although the body of the forms is rounded. Exaggerated thick/thin contrasts weight the bowls of the letters at a low angle. The slashing verticals and flourished tails cut through the

solid, even texture, which is created by the use of interlocking forms and repeated letters. All these elements have been carefully thought out in the arrangement of the alphabet as a complete design form. The fluid tracks of the broad-nibbed pen show how the practiced calligrapher can invest simple letterforms with a lively spontaneity while preserving an overall balance.

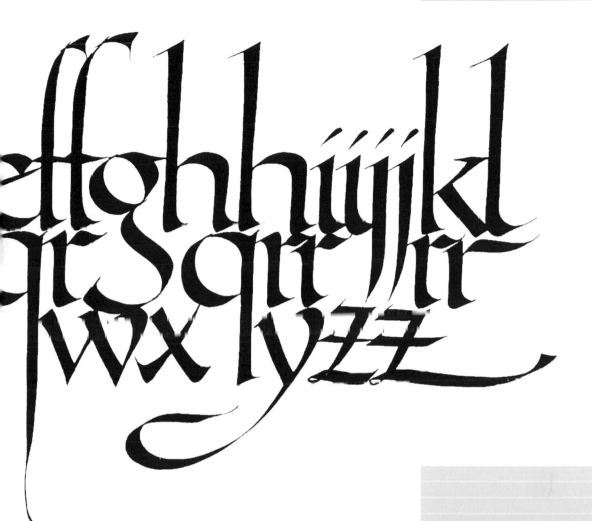

This lively Roman lower-case lettering emphasizes the pattern value of letterforms, drawn very freely, although designed *en bloc*.

Uncial and Half-uncial

There are many early Greek examples of this ancient letterform and the use of Uncials spread to the Roman Empire while Roman square and Rustic capitals were still in use. The "new" hand provided some economy of strokes and more speed, but it retained formality. The Romans gave it the name Uncial, from *uncia* (meaning "inch"). A study of early Christian manuscripts shows that it became the main book hand of the medieval period.

The Uncial hand is upright and bold, with full and rounded letters. It has an uncomplicated construction sequence with, at times, only a mere hint of the existence of ascenders and descenders. The best tools for writing Uncials are a broad nib or square-tipped brush. The nib gives a clean, sharp outer edge to the letters.

OLD VERSUS NEW

The old style of very round Uncials was made with the pen held almost horizontally, using a letter height of three to four nib widths. The modern, more open style is executed with a pen angle of 10°–20° and a height of five nib widths. The clubbed serifs are made by

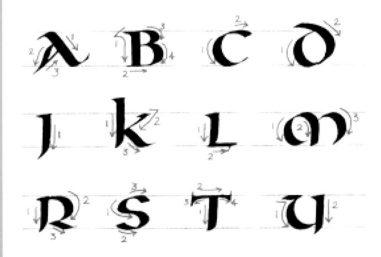

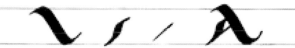

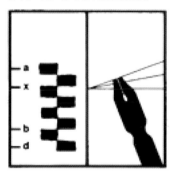

The stroke diagram clearly shows the quite delicate nature of the second stroke of the letter.

forming a small angled stroke followed by the upright stroke. Some Uncials can be given a hairline serif as an extension of a non-enclosed stroke.

Spacing between the letters of this rotund hand requires some special attention. Each letter should be able to "breathe." Try to achieve a balance of black and white, increasing the spaces between words and lines as necessary.

When you see a page of Uncials, you get an overwhelming sense of the letters being compressed neatly between parallel lines. The need to combine Uncials with another hand frequently arises, to develop the texture of the work. Versals are the natural complement to this quite adaptable hand of thin horizontals and thick verticals.

UNCIAL ALPHABET

The Uncial majuscule letters above are written with the pen held at the very flat angle of 10°–20° to the horizontal.

Some calligraphers find this angle difficult and somewhat uncomfortable to execute.

Uncial letters are typically round and squat, with minimal ascenders and descenders. The serif is a small wedge, formed by a slightly angled stroke, which is followed by the upright stroke. It is best to use a broad nib or square-cut brush to form these letters, making special note of the fine, thin lines that offset the thick strokes.

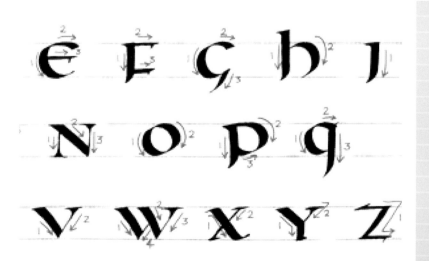

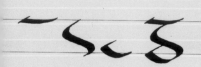

HALF-UNCIAL ALPHABET

The Half-uncial majuscule is closely identified with Anglo-Saxon and Celtic insular hands. The letters are four to four-and-a-half widths in height, with a flat pen angle. The letterforms are round, and have short descenders and ascenders, the latter with a distinctive wedge-shaped serif. The interlinear spacing can be kept to a minimum, although well-considered spacing between the lines creates a fine image overall. Spacing the lines by as much as four or more nib widths allows room for a single letter at the beginning of a sentence to be enlarged and decorated. These letters are excellent forms to decorate.

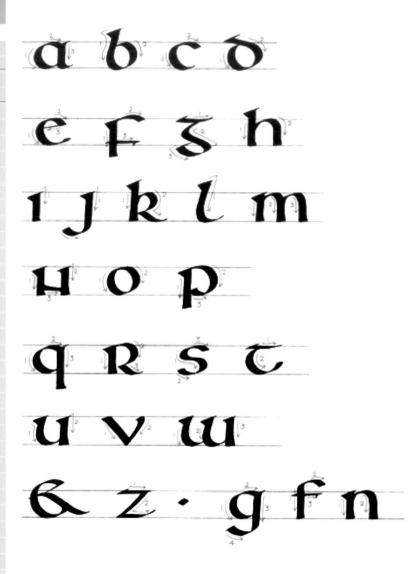

HALF-UNCIAL LETTERING

With its minimal ascenders and descenders, the Uncial is regarded as a majuscule hand. The Half-uncial, although still seen as a majuscule, is often accredited as the forerunner of most minuscule forms.

The ascenders and descenders distinctly rise and fall from the bodies of the letters, making an immediate association with lower-case letters. The Uncial and Half-uncial are acknowledged as the inspiration for the Celtic insular script that was used to produce Ireland's most famous manuscript, the *Book of Kells*.

If you have difficulty making the first stroke, divide the task into two strokes (see diagram top left). Make the long horizontal stroke first, and then add a small stroke on the left-hand top edge. The main stroke of the letter may need some practice to achieve the correct balance of open and closed counter strokes after the application of the final stroke.

FORMING UNCIAL LETTERS

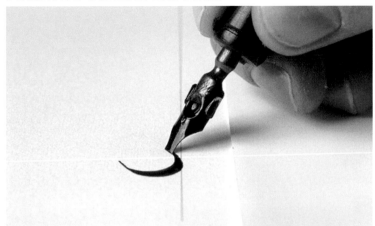

1 Uncial is a broad face, the pen being held at a very flat angle of 10°–20° to obtain the broad downstroke.

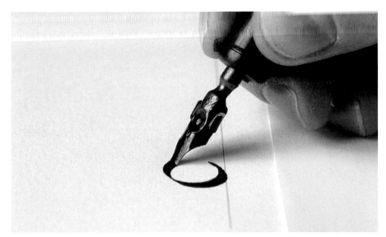

2 The pen is lifted from the paper before drawing the broad top stroke of the G.

3 The slimmer tail stroke is added. This face is characterized by full, rounded letters with very short ascenders and descenders.

MODERN UNCIAL

The curving shapes of Uncial letters were more rapidly and easily written with an edged pen than were the angular capitals of Roman letters.

Uncials therefore became the main book hand of the late Roman Empire and the primary form in Christian manuscripts up until the eighth century.

A number of variations arose in the design of individual letters: particularly in A, D, H, M, N, T, and W (see opposite), where there are alternative forms that roughly correspond to the typically differentiated identities of subsequent capital and minuscule alphabets.

Uncials are generally fairly heavy letters written with the flat edge of a square-tipped pen. But, as can be seen from the written sample, they form an immensely rich and descriptive texture, all the more elegant for the finely hooked terminals and the hairline flourishes.

The first stroke of this letter should capture the roundness of the letter shape—based on the o. The second stroke completes this round quality. Finally, the tail of the letter is added.

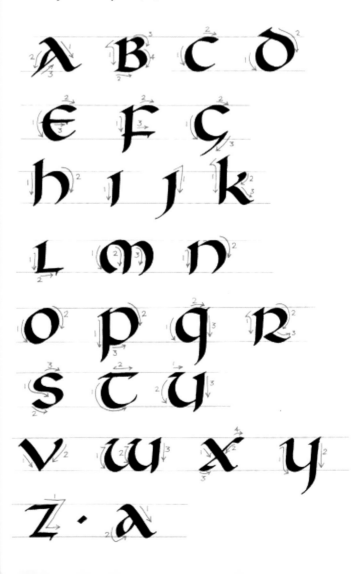

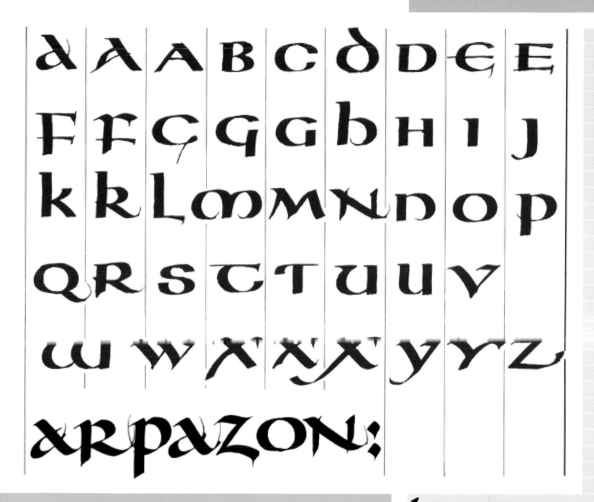

MODERN UNCIAL ALPHABET

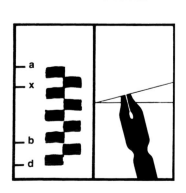

Derived from the traditional Uncial majuscule, the letters of modern Uncial are quite heavy, and maintain the roundness of all the other Uncial forms.

The letters are written with a flat pen angle of 15° to the horizontal, although an angle of 30° is acceptable. The letter height is four-and-a-half to five nib widths. The short ascenders and descenders of Uncial hands are maintained. Many of the vertical strokes and descenders taper off to the left, with no serif.

These letterforms seem to have a universal appeal, perhaps because of their rich round shapes. Their weight is strong: about four nib widths to the height. The Uncial is very adaptable and, although the pen is usually held horizontally, it can also produce other characteristics when drawn at an angle.

ENGLISH UNCIALS AND HALF-UNCIALS

This alphabet shows another modern transcription of the early Uncial form, followed by a Half-uncial alphabet, the book hand that followed on from Uncials. In this case, the Half-uncials are based on early English lettering from the beautifully decorated Lindisfarne Gospels, written in the seventh century. In the Half-uncials, the characteristics leading to minuscule, or lower-case, forms

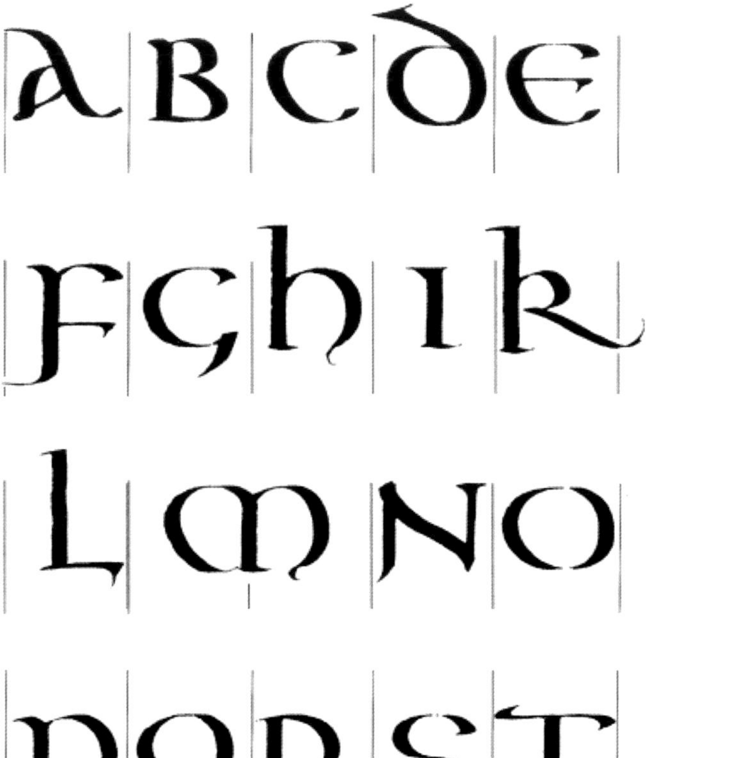

ABCDE

FGHIK

LMNO

PQRST

UVWXY

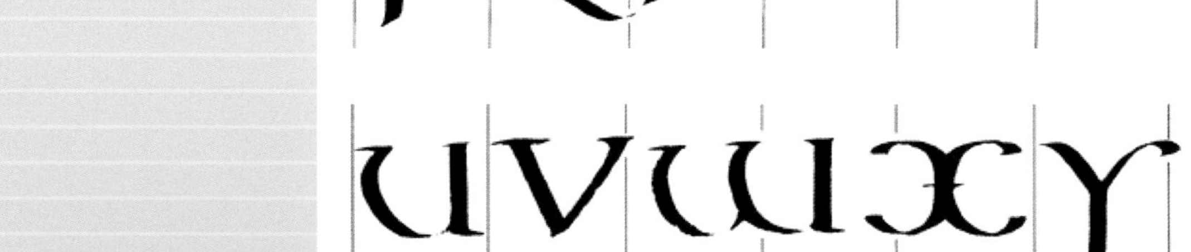

Pater noster,qui

are readily apparent. This is a systematic and formal script, with deliberate ascenders and descenders breaking out of the body height of the letters. Despite the lingering reference to the capital form of N, this is otherwise the precursor of lower-case forms, and it is particularly noticeable that the semi-capitalized A still in use in the Uncial alphabet has been completely modified into the more rounded, compact character appropriate to the Half-uncial script.

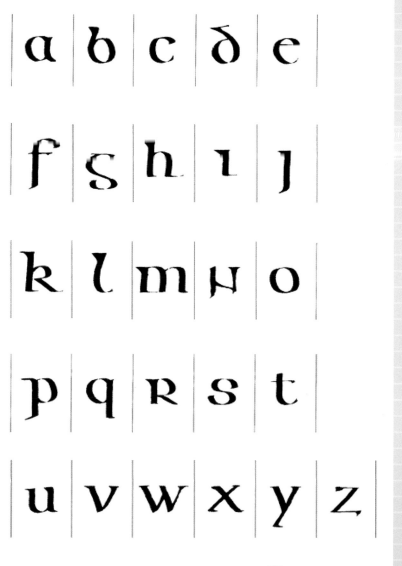

est in coelis:sancti

Versal Alphabets

These elegant capital letters appear liberally throughout early manuscripts, but were seldom used to compose an entire block of text. Sometimes emblazoned beyond recognition, their main purpose was to serve as chapter openings, to draw attention to an important section of the text, or to begin a paragraph or verse. There were no minuscule forms, so the accompanying body of text would be executed in Uncial, Half-uncial, or Carolingian letters.

I n medieval times, Versal letters used as initials were simply colored green, red, or blue. Richly burnished gold versions were limited to use in manuscripts deemed of particular importance.

The unusual feature of Versals in calligraphic terms is that they are built-up, not written letters. The construction appears straightforward, but it is curiously difficult to master. Most of the strokes are formed in the same way, whether they are curved or straight. As a guide to height, base the letter on eight to ten times the width of the letter's stem.

It is advisable to begin by drawing a light pencil outline, so that the correct angles and counter shapes are established. Then you can work the letter stroke by stroke using a medium-fine pen, starting with the uprights. These are slightly "waisted," tapering inward to the center and broadening a little at the ends. The diagonal strokes are similarly constructed. Unless you are adding color, a single stroke should fill in the letter once the outlines have been drawn. The slightly extended hairline serifs are formed with the pen held flat.

ROUNDED COUNTERS

Letters with rounded counters should fall slightly above and below the actual letter height. When making these letters, complete the inner line of the counter first, so that you achieve the correct proportions. The outer curves of the letters are slightly sharper than the inner ones. In letters that have cross-bars, these are placed above the middle.

The spaciousness of these graceful letterforms provides much scope for decoration. You can add a contrasting color simply by using a pen or brush to make the filling-in stroke.

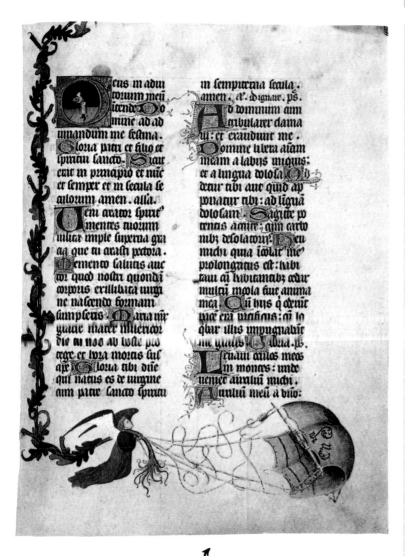

↑
In the Egerton manuscript, patterns and fine lines decorate the Lombardic Versal letters. The strong influence of Uncial letter shapes is also clear.

A heading, or the first word of a text, catches attention when it is richly embellished with color, has hairlines added, and has elaborate flourishes swirled into intricate patterns. Beginning a piece of work with a single versal also offers an excellent opportunity for gilding.

Contemporary design trends have provided new perceptions of works composed entirely of upper-case letters. The elegant Versal works well in many contexts. A rhythmic texture can be created if careful consideration is given to the spaces the letters occupy. To achieve movement in the design, some of the letters may vary in size, but maintaining a constant letter size can result in a work of great elegance.

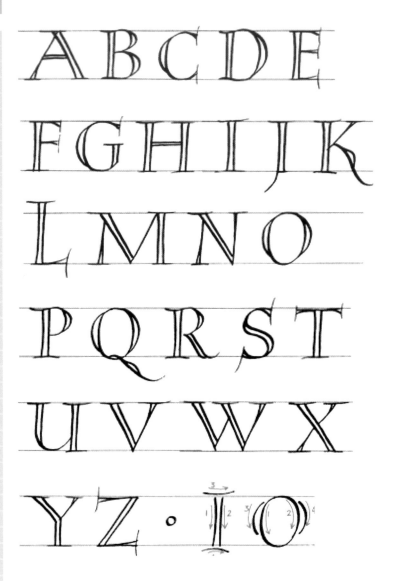

VERSAL ALPHABET

These built-up capital letters are excellent forms for headings and decorating, and work well with many calligraphic hands.

The inner strokes are drawn first to ensure the counter shape is the correct proportion. The waisted vertical strokes are constructed with great care; the waisting is a subtle curve and must not be exaggerated.

A metal nib, or a fine, pointed lettering brush or quill can be used to construct these letters. Whichever instrument you choose, it is manipulated at various angles to achieve a balance of both thin and thick strokes.

The slightly waisted vertical strokes of the letter are drawn first (see left). Turn the pen to 0° to the horizontal writing line, and draw the serifs. Draw the inner stroke of the counter to establish the shape, then the outer strokes are added.

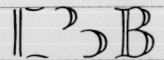

FORMING VERSAL LETTERS

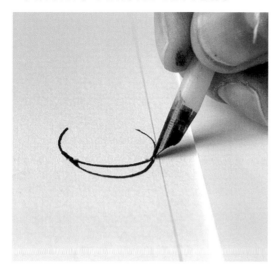

1 In this Versal capital E, the inner stroke is drawn first to establish the shape of the counter, and then the outer stroke is drawn. (On straight downstrokes, the stroke is slightly waisted in the middle.)

2 The two middle cross-strokes start at the width of the nib and are splayed in two flaring strokes at the end to produce a wedge shape.

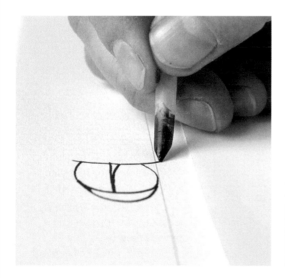

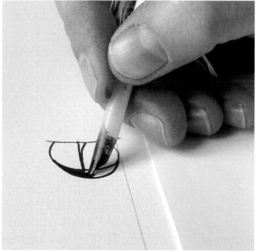

3 The enclosing downstroke is now drawn. These hairline strokes should be lightly drawn, with the pen held at a 90° angle.

4 The skeleton lettering is filled in with a single stroke. Filling in can also be done with a fine sable brush.

Versals are essentially pen-made with a flexible quill or metal pen. Each Versal letter is actually formed with three strokes: a vertical stem, for example, is outlined on each side, and the third stroke is quickly applied to fill the space between.

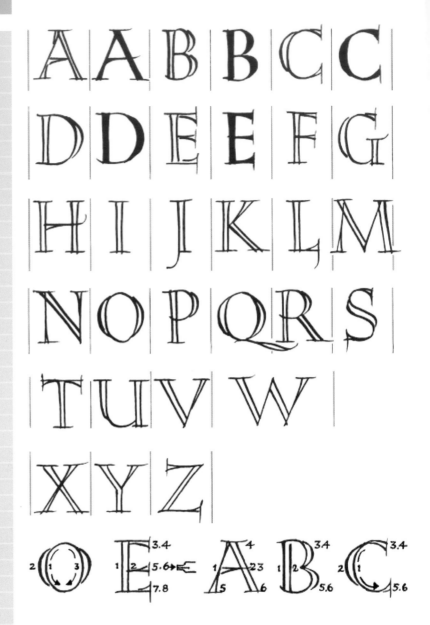

VERSALS— ROMAN FORM

These simple Versals are in a style based on Roman capitals, as commonly used in early manuscripts. The important characteristic of Versals, compared with other calligraphic lettering, is that the letterforms are built up gradually rather than written fluidly. The pen is narrower and more flexible than that used to write the text. In this sample, fine hairline serifs complete the forms; these are in lieu of the Roman serif.

VERSALS— LOMBARDIC FORM

The curving shapes of this Versal alphabet are influenced by both Lombardic scripts and Uncial letters, as is demonstrated particularly in the forms of D, H, and M. The cross-strokes and curves are terminated with a flaring of the width cut across by a hairline, and these lines are rather more bold and flourished than in the Roman-style Versals, creating a lively textural rhythm.

The fine, flexible quill or pen used to draw the Versals can be charged with ink or thinned watercolor paint. Two-color Versals can be attractively made by drawing the outer strokes in a dark ink and flooding the inner area with a strong color.

These are richer forms of Versals, largely based on Uncial letters, producing free and lively expression and used continuously throughout the ages.

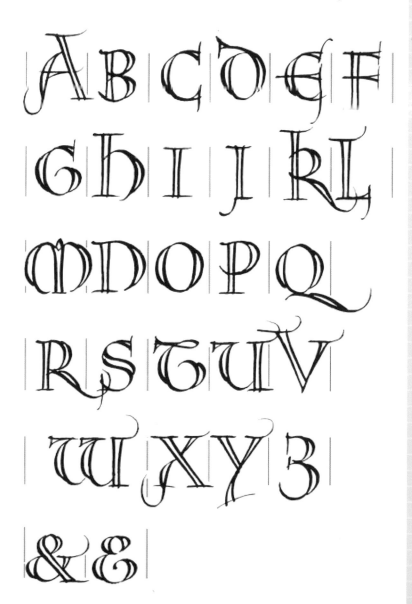

ELABORATED VERSALS

The design of this alphabet takes the rhythmic and flourished quality of the Lombardic style a little further. The construction of the letterforms is very fluid and decorative, from the exaggerated tails of K, Q, R, and X, to the individual details enlivening the counter spaces of B, O, and Q. The elaboration is of a consistent style and quality, but intriguingly varied in detail to make the lettering clearly legible.

The form of each letter in Elaborated Versal is not only easy to distinguish, but individually ornamental.

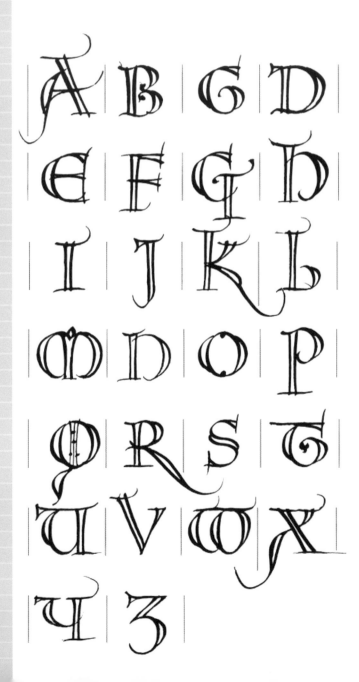

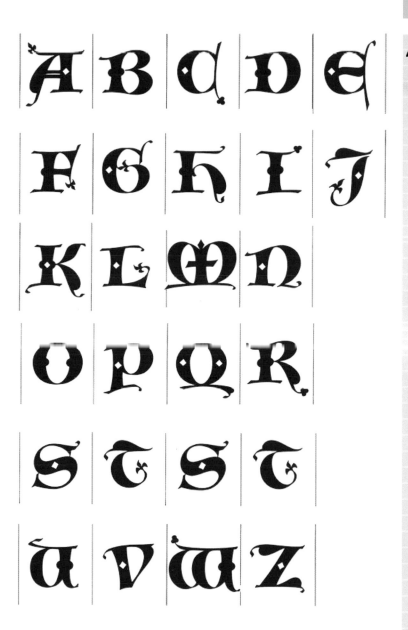

This style of heavy ornamentation on Versal capitals was very popular in medieval manuscripts.

ORNAMENTED VERSALS

The weighty shapes of these Lombardic-style Versals are sufficiently broad to allow a decorative piercing of the curves and stems, in addition to flourished and ornamental detail. The drawn Versal letter can be the basis of a heavily ornamented or illuminated capital letter, decorated with abstract motifs or, as in the original miniatures of medieval manuscripts, with tiny pictures of figurative images.

Colors can be introduced to add variety to the design, and Versals are also traditionally the subjects for gilding, with burnished gold leaf or painted powder gold.

Gothic Alphabets

Numerous styles of lettering evolved during the Gothic era—the period broadly straddling the twelfth to sixteenth centuries. Developments in writing reflected changes of style in the built environment, where lancet arches replaced the rounded Roman arches, and ribbed vaults and thrusting flying buttresses appeared.

I n the medieval period, a wide variety of Gothic hands emerged, sharing many common elements, including a heavy, dense black form, angular letters, rigid verticals, and, often, short ascenders and descenders in relation to the height.

ANGULARITY

Sometimes the emphasis on angularity renders the work almost illegible to modern readers. The many variations, both formal and informal, are attributable to the numbers of people who adapted the forms to suit their own requirements. Often small changes in structure occurred simply through the need for speed and economy in writing.

Some rounded versions of Gothic lettering did persist and develop, such as Rotunda. Other Gothic forms practiced today are Blackletter and Textura.

With due consideration, Gothic lettering can be very effective. To use it successfully, plan the piece carefully and do plenty of rough workings, developing your ability to space the letters consistently. When working on the final piece, make sure you execute the strokes with determination.

A Gothic hand can be produced using a broad pen held at an angle of 45°, and by using a height of five nib widths. If you use a height of six nib widths, you achieve a more slender letter with greater clarity.

A neat and textured work results from making the white spaces within and between the letters the same thickness as upright strokes.

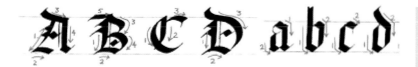

UPPER AND LOWER CASE

Originally, there were no specific capital letters in the Gothic forms. Usually, a decorated letter was dropped in, and this worked surprisingly well. The Gothic upper case now used is distinctly open, even rounded, compared with the lower-case lettering. The height is seven nib widths. Gothic capitals work best on their own as individual letters Seldom nowadays are they used successfully for an entire word.

In the lower-case letters, a square serif is used which sits atop the strokes. In the upper-case forms, the same square serifs are seen, but they are more usually sited on the left-hand outside edge of the upright strokes.

BLACKLETTER

Like so many developments in writing, Blackletter was born of a need for speed and economy. The style is composed of thrusting, upright strokes that create an overall vertical effect, but the eye can find rest in the horizontals breaking the spaces at top and bottom of the letters.

To write this hand, you hold a broad pen at an angle of 30°–40° to the writing line. The weight of the letter can be varied by adjusting the height between three and five nib widths. The counter spaces, the vertical strokes, and the spaces

between the letters are usually of identical thickness.

Blackletter is very economical, because constant condensing means that it is possible to have more letters per line and more words per page. The spaces between lines can be reduced, and the ascenders and descenders shortened to a minimum to create a very dense texture. This occurs in the version of Gothic lettering that is known as Textura (see page 144), which can be seen as a pure pattern.

The upper-case letters, seven nib widths in height, are not conducive to use in whole words, as legibility becomes a problem.

This Gothic hand works surprisingly well with decorative capitals, and there are many fine historical examples.

GOTHIC BLACKLETTER ALPHABET

The upper-case letters of seven nib widths in height have a roundness that contrasts well with the angularity of the lower-case letters of five nib widths height. The distinctive, angular o, for example, is a good guide for the lower-case letters. The short ascenders and descenders permit tight interlinear spacing.

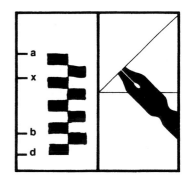

A B C D E
F G H I J
K L M N O
P Q R S T U
U W E Y Z
a b c d e f g h
i j k l m n o p
q r s t u v w
x y z · a n v s

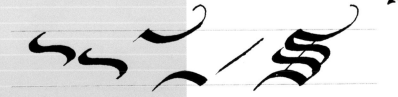

This splendid Gothic S is easier to execute than appears on first viewing. Breaking it down into its constituent parts to work out how it is made, it transpires that it is constructed of similar strokes traveling in the same direction, as the stroke diagram illustrates.

FORMING GOTHIC LETTERS

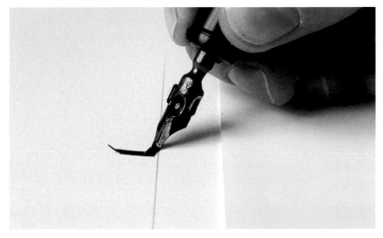

1 The first stroke of this Blackletter g is formed by holding the pen at an angle of 35° and making a fine line diagonally to the left. Almost immediately the pen is pulled down into the strong vertical line. Before this stroke reaches the baseline, it is stopped and a strong diagonal stroke is pulled down to the right and onto the baseline.

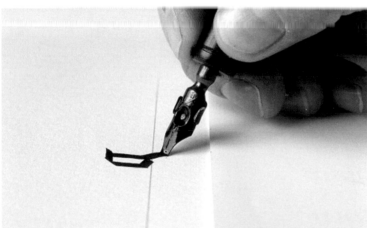

2 The pen returns to the top of the letter, and rests at the pen angle where the first stroke began. The pen is pulled to the right, beyond where the next vertical line will begin. The vertical stroke that becomes the descender curves out to the right before it reaches the baseline. At about two nib widths below the baseline, the stroke is pulled back to the left, and to the thinnest part of the stroke, where it stops.

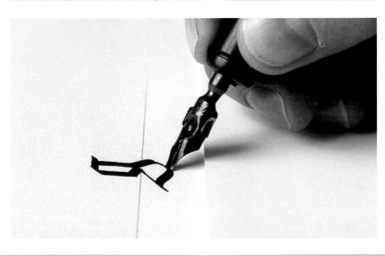

3 The final stroke begins with a hairline drawn from the end of the diagonal stroke resting on the baseline. It travels down to the left. To complete the descender, a wave stroke is made to the right, where it joins up with the middle of the descender.

GOTHIC CURSIVE ALPHABET

This elegant hand is perhaps less well known and therefore not widely used. A single upper-case letter used with lower-case letters can be used for a heading with eye-catching effect. The lower-case letters are written four-and-a-half to five nib widths high.

The letters are pointed where they touch the baseline, and some have fine line extensions from this point. Some of the descenders end in sharp fine line extended strokes. The upper-case letters are written six-and-a-half to seven nib widths high. Many of these capital letters are more recognizable as lower-case forms. It is evident, when looking at the lower-case letters, that this hand evolved to be written at speed.

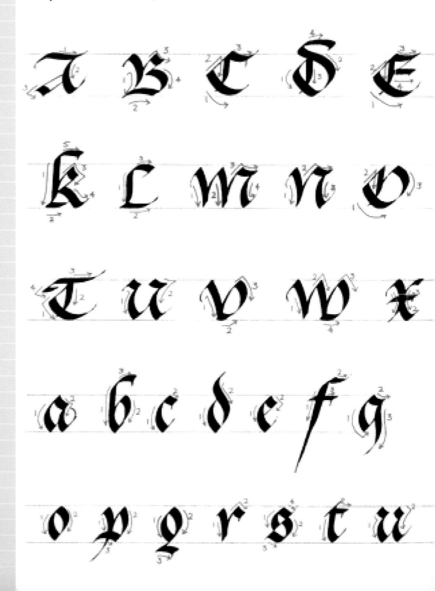

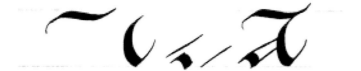

The Gothic cursive upper-case A is presented in a shape more recognizable as a lower-case letter. The cross-stroke, which begins the letter at the top, holds and balances the rest of the letter. The fine lines must contrast with the bold strokes to give this hand its own particular identity.

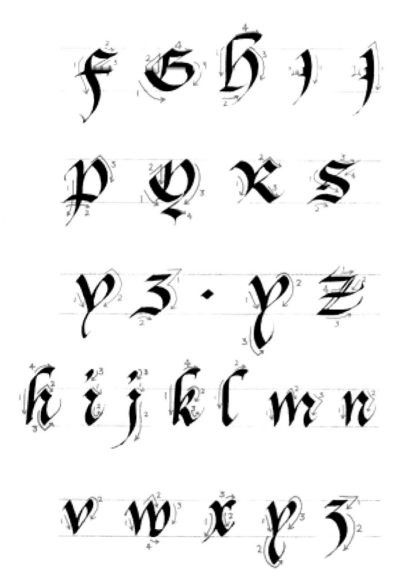

The letters have a distinctive almond (mandorla) shape thought to have been a western Asian influence.

ROTUNDA (ROTONDA)

Variously referred to as Italian Gothic, half-Gothic, or round Gothic, this crisp hand was used as a book hand in medieval and Renaissance Italy.

In northern Europe, the hard, dense Blackletter style flourished, but in the southern countries there was a distinctly softer form, especially by comparison with the compact and angular Textura, a style never seriously pursued in Italy. However, a further comparison with the Gothic hands practiced in the north reveals that there is a slight angularity in the spaciousness of Rotunda, which is particularly pronounced on letters with enclosed counter spaces.

Medieval Italian manuscripts show the form exquisitely. The ascenders and descenders are often minimal, which creates an even, linear texture. The space

ROTUNDA MINUSCULE ALPHABET

The Rotunda minuscule is a more open and rounded Gothic hand. The letters are written four-and-a-half to five nib widths high, and with a pen angle of 30° to the horizontal. The letters maintain some of the obvious Gothic characteristics. The ascenders and descenders are short, but the distinctive lozenge-shaped serif is seldom used. Many of the letters have strokes that have square endings. There is a distinct softening of stroke compared with the more familiar angularity of some other Gothic hands.

Rotunda minuscules need practice to obtain the roundness of the counter shapes, and still retain the slight angularity of the corners so typical of Gothic hands.

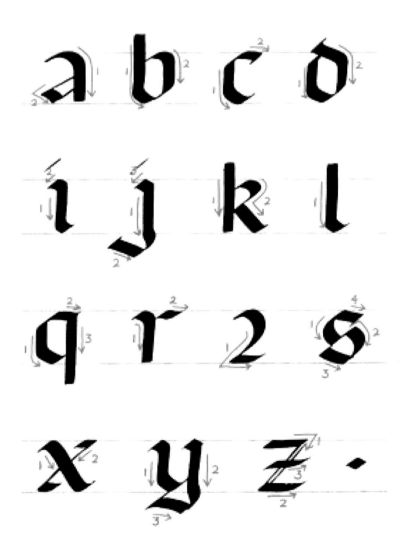

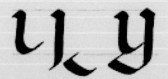

between both letters and words is often pronounced, but there still exists a balanced structure of bold, upright strokes and fine, thin strokes.

SERIFS

The serif style varied according to the preference of the scribe. Fine hairline extensions are often applied, and many strokes simply terminate with the pen angle. There are a few examples that show the use of the truly Gothic-style lozenge-shaped serif.

The simple, clean letters need to be carefully formed in order to display their pleasing proportions. The letters are written with a pen angle of 30°.

Some early manuscripts include pen-drawn capitals constructed in a similar manner to letters in the body of the text, but they are more rounded.

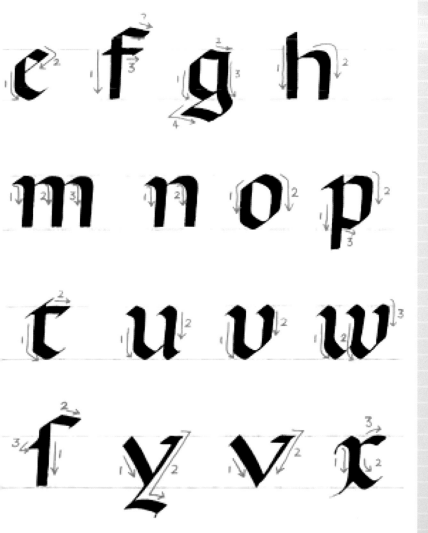

This rounded, open hand was skillfully combined with lavishly illuminated Versals (see page 128).

TEXTURA

This Gothic script, which was mostly practiced in northern Europe, takes its name from the Latin *textum*, meaning "woven fabric" or "texture." Used as a book hand and widely found in early psalters and prayer books, this lower-case alphabet developed in many formal and informal styles. Two of the formal hands were *textus precissus* and *textus quadratus*. The former was characterized by strong upright strokes standing flat on the baseline; the latter by distinctive diamond-shaped serifs and forking at the tops of the ascenders.

The Textura hand, as its name suggests, is built of condensed, bold black verticals. These are identical in thickness to the counter spaces and the spaces between the letters. The spacing between lines is minimal, which is ideal for accommodating the typically Gothic short ascenders and descenders.

Textura alphabet: the forms of Gothic script, known as Blackletter, are instantly recognizable from the compressed, angular, and vertically stressed letters. The original proportions of Textura were based on three strokes of the pen, so that the interior spaces were the same width as the pen strokes. This version shows a slightly more open form with serifs.

Fraktur alphabet: less angular than the Gothic Textura, yet equally characteristic of its time, is the Blackletter script known as Fraktur, which is identifiable by its forked ascenders. This curious branching of the vertical stroke derived from the cutting of a quill pen with the tip slit to one side rather than centrally, so a slight flick of the pen would create an unevenly broken terminal.

To execute this hand, you hold the broad nib at 40°. The letter height is six nib widths. Variations in height create further interest in the texture of the overall design.

The letters have a distinct angular stress. Extra hairlines can be added by lifting one corner of the pen at the end of a stroke and dragging a little wet ink outward to become the hairline extension.

A recognizable feature of manuscripts written in Textura is the line filling. Where a line finished short of the right-hand margin, the scribe would complete the line with exquisite patterning. If the line was short by only one or two letters, a simple flourish or pen pattern would serve the purpose. This is a solution that can be utilized for many design problems.

The patterning must pay respect to the lettering style: thus, for Textura, it must be quite solid.

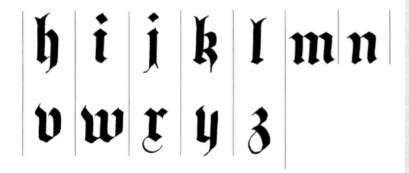

GOTHIC MAJUSCULE

These majuscule letters are noticeably rounded and open in form, texturally far less dense and heavy than other styles corresponding to the Blackletter script. This suggests that the alphabet derives from capital letters used as decorative initials, since the strokes are of medium weight by reference to the body size of the letterforms, providing interior spaces sufficiently open to allow for ornamentation of the form. They include pen-drawn decoration in the features

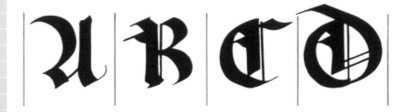

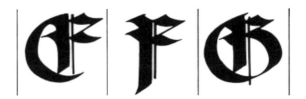

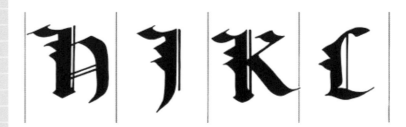

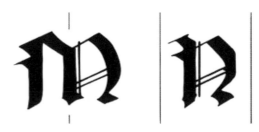

extending from the structural outlines—small flicked protrusions and double hairlines attached to the counters and vertical stems. The curving strokes show the influence of Lombardic and Uncial lettering (see page 120).

An unusually light alphabet, the capitals have a filigree detail. The Uncial influence is clearly seen in the U and M.

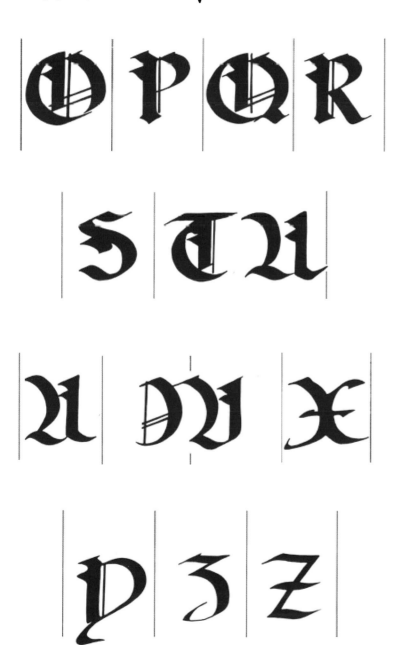

MODIFIED GOTHIC CAPITALS

A modern revision of Blackletter styling gives these capital letters a squared and open character, combined with the rich, black texture of Gothic—yet gives a more pronounced variation between thick and thin strokes.

There is some influence from the basic constructions of Uncial letters; and although these are relatively simple, broadly described shapes, they have a sophisticated style and consistency derived from the well-judged proportions and the economy of the pen movements.

Modified Gothic capitals: tiny twists and flourishes of the pen give the curving stems and bowls a lively rhythm.

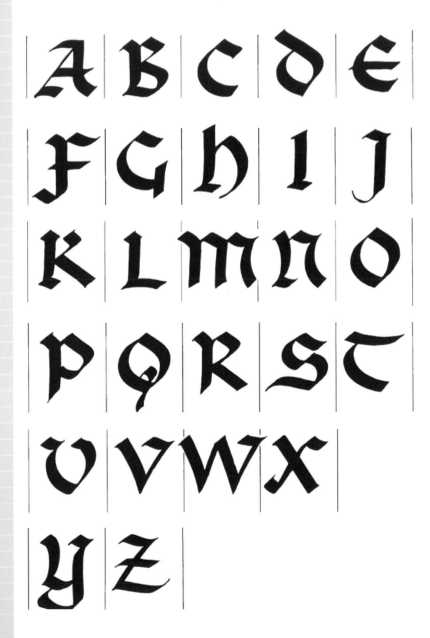

MODIFIED GOTHIC SCRIPT

A simplified version of a rounded Gothic script corresponds to the capital letters in the sample. Here again, the influence of Uncial letters is visible in the forms of d and h, for example, and the compactness of the forms is maintained by the shortened descenders in p and q. Although a formalized style with the typically dense texture of Gothic scripts, this alphabet has a variation in the letter construction that makes it a much more distinct and legible script for most readers than the more stylized, angular Textura.

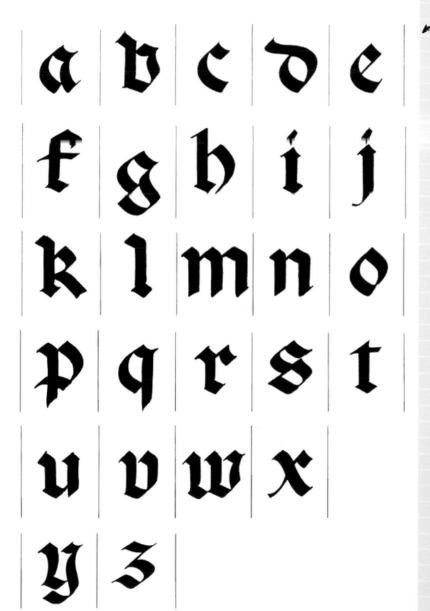

Modified Gothic script: this is a heavily weighted yet distinct style.

A heavy, decorative Gothic letter with the unusual feature of a base loop, making a rich textural effect.

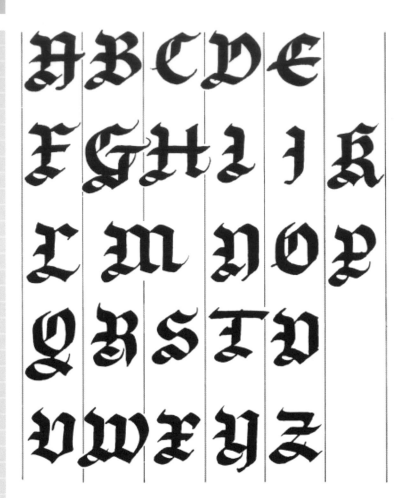

DECORATED GOTHIC CAPITALS

This alphabet is a modern version of capital lettering based on features of Gothic style. Although not an authentic historical form, it is constructed from the elements of the original Blackletter, but with a loosely curving and flourished manner that creates a more elaborate patterning through the forms.

The letters are regularly proportioned and designed in logical relation one to another, enlivened by rhythmic motion in the vigorous pen strokes and controlled flourishes. The looping of stems and tails is carried through consistently, adding to the richness of the textural quality. The broken counters of D, O, and Q relate to an ornamental device often seen in illuminated Gothic capitals.

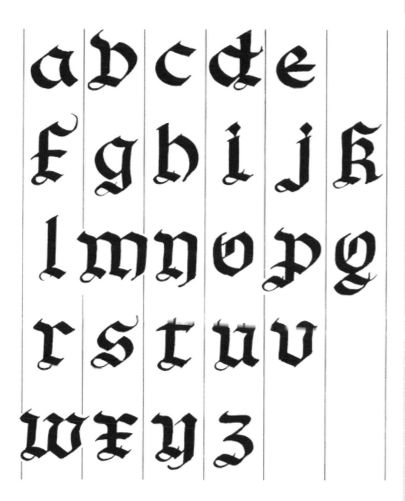

The accompanying small letter
of the alphabet shown opposite
maintains the characteristic loop
of the capital forms.

DECORATED GOTHIC MINUSCULE

Following from the decorated capital letters, the minuscule form corresponding to the previous example shows the same generously curving construction. The elaboration extends into the unusual curling tails and ascenders and the brief, finely flourished loops attached to the vertical stems of certain letters. The generally heavy, even texture of the alphabet is inspired by the authentic Blackletter forms. The characteristics of Gothic script are clearly seen in m and w—although these letters are here more widely proportioned than is typical in the original style on which they are based.

The skeleton forms of this Fraktur-based letter, German in origin, create a light and airy effect. The large initial letters would produce a suitable foil for a simpler text.

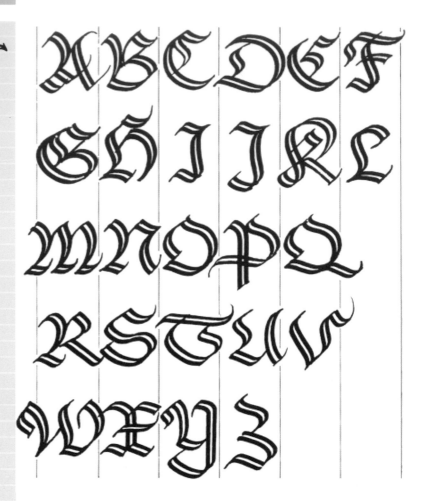

SKELETON GOTHIC CAPITALS

This modern revision of capital letters, loosely based on the style of Fraktur, is written with a double-stroke pen to form an even, open pattern. The double stroke demonstrates clearly the basic form of each letter and the variation between thick and thin occurring naturally in the pen strokes according to the direction of the pen. In this case, the thick/thin modulation appears as a transition from a double to a single line. Fraktur has a ragged quality echoed in the pointed tails and terminals of these letters. The Gothic origin of the style is apparent in the heavily bowed T and the horizontal crossbar of X. The curling elaboration of the forms is appropriately applied, and despite the patterned quality of the design, each letter retains its recognizable identity.

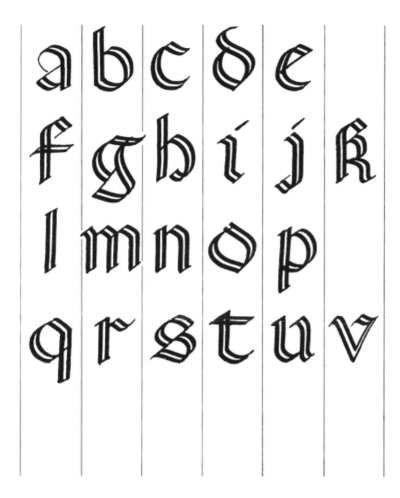

SKELETON GOTHIC MINUSCULE

Script letters form the bulk of a text and are characteristically less elaborate than their capital counterparts because of the need for legibility. In these minuscules, the termination of the strokes is relatively abrupt; the tails and ascenders, as in d and g, minimally flourished. Outlining of the form relieves the heavy textural density that is typically a feature of Gothic lettering. Though the letters, composed mainly of straight strokes, still have a degree of angularity, the overall design is broad and open, the counters generously rounded. This feature is typical of later Gothic scripts, in the forms known as Bastarda and Rotunda.

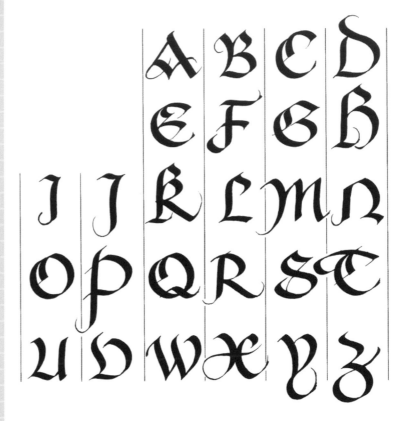

MODIFIED GOTHIC CURSIVE CAPITALS

The cursive quality in lettering is similar to that of ordinary handwriting.

Letterforms are written with a fairly rapid traveling motion rather than the precision and order needed to maintain the more formal styles. The modern alphabet based on Gothic cursive capitals is a highly designed form with a logical structure and proportional system, but the vigor and fluidity of the writing gives the letterforms a delightful spontaneity. Lightly flourished hooks and curves contribute to this quality and indicate the movement of the pen along the writing line.

There are elements of italic styling in the branched arches of M and the lively points of W, but this is an upright rather than slanted form and the speed of cursive writing is more fully incorporated in the development of compressed and slanted italics.

a b c d
e f g h
j k l m n
o p q r s t
u v w x y z
1 2 3 4 5 6 7 8 9

MODIFIED GOTHIC CURSIVE SCRIPT

This widely influential running hand of the Gothic period was notable for the almond-shaped O, which was borrowed from western Asian sources and taken to Europe following the Crusades. In this modified revision of Gothic cursive script, the almond (mandorla) shape influences the construction of all the curved and bowed letters.

Compared with the capital alphabet, the script is obliquely written so that the letters readily become linked when a text is written at speed. The numerals are simply designed, with the same fluid, rhythmic quality as the letterforms.

Italic Alphabets

The Italic hand developed in Renaissance Italy. There was a need for greater speed in writing, particularly for copying large amounts of text. Through studies of classical manuscripts of the ninth century, Italian scholars evolved this compressed and more than usually slanting style. The compression is based on an elliptical o. The Italic alphabet is a good model as a first hand to learn.

In the Italic hand, a broad pen held at an angle of 45° achieves the characteristic contrast of thick and thin strokes. The hand has simple serifs and ascenders and descenders that can be varied in length. Simple or elaborate flourishing and swashes can be introduced as an extension to many letters (see page 159).

Together, these characteristics constitute a truly elegant hand that, with practice, should retain its graceful proportions even when written at speed. These are the factors that render the formal Italic hand so suitable for use as the basis for many fine handwriting styles in common use today.

The height of the lower-case letters is five nib widths, of the upper-case letters, seven nib widths. Ascenders and descenders are usually about three to four nib widths. A lighter weight can be achieved by increasing the lower-case letter height to six nib widths.

Italic letterforms work well in many situations. The style is excellent for work that needs to be easily read and comprehended. It has a curious ability to be appropriate in both formal and informal settings.

Blocks of text rendered in Italic can be given textural variation by the introduction of another hand, for example, Foundational, for headings and sub-headings.

With the addition of suitable flourishing, menus, name cards, invitations, and certificates can be rendered as designs of character and elegance without loss of legibility. Try not to overdo the amount of flourishing: too much makes the lettering difficult to read and less pleasing to the viewer.

There is plenty of room for inventiveness, such as

A B C D E F F G H I J K L M

N O P Q R S T U V W X Y Z

a b c d e f g h i j k l m n o p

q r s t u v w x y z · f g r y

l̓k I k̓ K

An important feature of the lower-case letters here is the way in which the arching stroke is made. The construction of the k, b, and p is similar to the h, m, and n. This construction shows how the serif can be written as an integral part of the first stroke, or the pen can be lifted off the paper and the serif added.

experimenting with double and connecting letters. The two main connectors are horizontal and diagonal lines. The object of the exercise is to achieve a join that appears to be a natural extension of the letters.

ITALIC ALPHABET

The lower-case letters of the italic alphabet are five nib widths in height and executed with the pen nib at a 45° angle.

The slant of the letters is maintained at an angle of 5°–10° to the vertical, depending on your personal preference. Whatever angle is selected, it must remain consistent throughout the work.

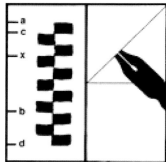

ITALIC LETTERING

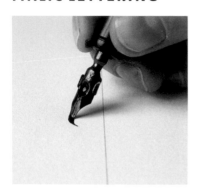

1 The elegant proportions of the Italic hand are achieved by maintaining a constant pen angle of 45°, and modeling the letters on the elliptical o. The letter g, shown here, shares the same characteristics as a, c, d, e, o, and q. The first stroke moves from the pen angle to the right. It is almost a straight stroke and forms the top of the letter.

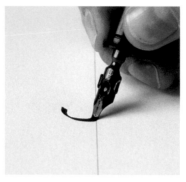

2 The second stroke begins at the same place as the first. It pulls around to form the first half of the elliptically shaped bowl of the letter.

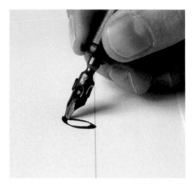

3 The stroke continues around until it reaches the thinnest part, and then climbs steeply toward the top of the letter.

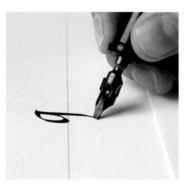

4 The backbone of the letter is the third stroke, which begins at the top, and plunges down into the descender. The stroke finishes in a slight curve to the left, which becomes the thinnest part of the stroke.

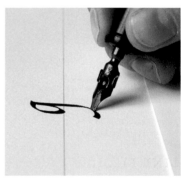

5 The last stroke of this letter starts in the white space to the left of the descender. The small finishing stroke is pulled to the right to meet the slightly curved end of the descender.

MAKING SWASHES

The Italic hand provides ideal basic letterforms for stroke extensions in the form of swashes. This selection can be used as a guide. Further interest can be created by the addition of hairline extensions to the swashes, but this needs to be done with caution.

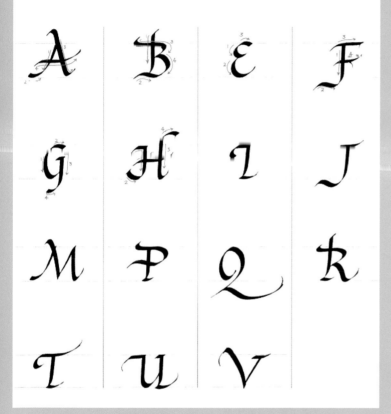

LINE FILLING

Another area for exploration while using Italic letterforms is where you find noticeable space between the last letter of a line and the natural end to that line. For example, the piece may not be justified on the right-hand margin, but too much white space may look out of place in the overall design, and you may wish to fill lines. You can approach this from two main directions.

The first approach is to extend the last letter—although this does not work with all letters. The second approach is to fill the line with a subtle border arrangement, such as dots made with the broad nib. For more ideas about borders, see pages 106–7.

ITALIC CAPITALS

Notably narrowed and slanted, these letters are a sophisticated modern Italic written with a consistent 45° pen angle that creates a fluid modulation in the strokes. Italic capitals are basically a compressed version of the Roman form and have a similar regularity of proportion governing the relationships between the different letters. Flowing extensions of the stems and tails break through the baseline to emphasize the elongated construction.

As the squared capitals were the characteristic formal lettering of the Roman Empire, so Italic was the typical pen form of scribes and scholars in Renaissance Italy.

The elegant capitals in this modern version of the Italic alphabet work well together. The length of flourishes on tails is optional.

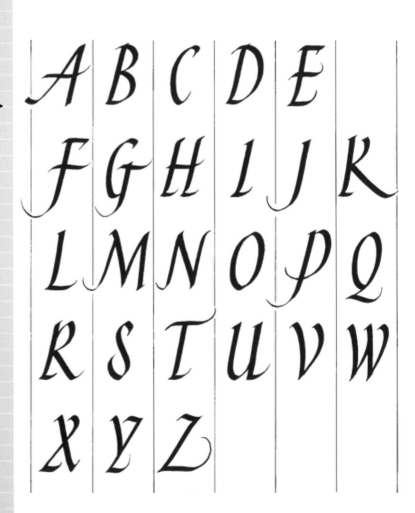

ITALIC LOWER CASE

Italic is a cursive hand, originally developed as a formal script that could be written rapidly without losing the fineness of its proportions and basic structure. In this version of the lower-case Italic alphabet, the curved ascenders and flourished descenders give greater emphasis to the slanting of the letters.

The extension of these strokes achieves a length slightly exceeding the body height of the letters, but it is not so exaggerated as to destroy the balance in the pattern of the lettering.

Apart from the slanting and compression of the letterforms, the main characteristic of Italic is the branching of the arches from the main stems in the letters h, m, and n. There is a similar construction in the bowls of b, k, and p, and this creates the angular nature of Italic script.

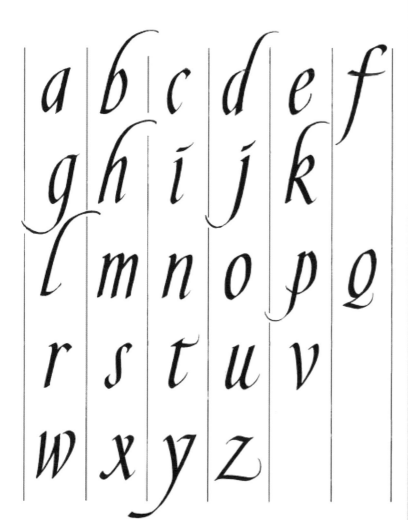

As with most Italics, these letters branch from the main stroke, and are compressed but consistent in width, with flowing ascenders and descenders.

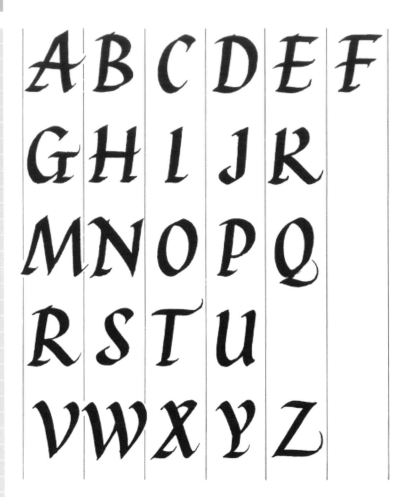

The capitals in another modern version of the Italic alphabet are tall and elegant and work well together.

ITALIC COMPRESSED HAND—CAPITALS

The compressed capital letters are compact forms of medium weight.

They have a clean and unelaborated style consistent with the lower-case letters, the same subtle slanting and oval counters being the characteristic qualities. The thick and thin variation of the movement of the edged pen is not particularly pronounced in these letterforms. Vertical and slanted strokes are begun with a slightly angled serif. The bases of the letters are neatly finished with hooked terminals or sturdy horizontal feet.

a b c d e f
g h i j k l
m n o p q
r s t u
v w x y z

These simple lower-case letters
are based on an oval, and the
pattern of the counter and
interspace should be drawn
as consistently as possible.
The arches are rounded,
rather than branched.

ITALIC COMPRESSED HAND—LOWER CASE

Compressed lettering is a
development from modern
reinterpretations of tenth-
century minuscule letters.

They are characteristically
elegant, simple forms, which
may be described as tilted but
not emphatically slanted. The
bowed letters are basically oval
rather than rounded or angular,
and this dictates the lateral
compression affecting the
proportions of the other letters.
Ascenders are finished with a
natural pen curve, as are the
descenders of g and y, while
in p and q, the dropped stems
are neatly terminated with a
sideways twist of the pen.

LITERA DA BREVI

A a b c d e e f g g h i k l m n o p q r s s t u x y z

~: Marcus Antonius Casanoua :~
Pierij vates, laudem si opera ista merentur,
Praxiteli nostro carmina pauca date'.
Non placet hoc; nostri pietas laudanda Coryti'est;
Qui dicat hæc; nisi vos forsan utercp mouet ;
Debetis saltem Dijs carmina, ni quoqs, et istis
Illa datis. iam nos mollia saxa sumus .

A A B B C C D D E E F F G G H H I
K L L M M N N O P P Q Q R R S
S T T U V V X X Y Z & & Bl Bl

Ludouicus Vicentinus scribebat Romæ' anno
salutis M D XXIII

Arrighi was a sixteenth-century Italian calligrapher living in Rome. He produced writing manuals and designed type, his Italic typefaces being the finest of the period. This is a reprint of his first copybook of 1522, based on the Humanist script.

COPYBOOK ITALIC

The Italic and Humanist scripts of the Renaissance were widely disseminated through the medium of printed copybooks, the first of which was published in 1522 by Ludovico degli Arrighi (d. 1527). This finely textured, even Italic is an extremely practical hand; the sample above appears to have been rapidly written without any loss to the elegance of the lettering.

It is interesting to note that, in the alphabet samples, the lower-case letters have a deliberate slant. Meanwhile the capitals alternate different versions—one of which is squared and upright in character, while the alternative form is compressed, elongated, and fluid.

FLOURISHED ITALIC

Although cursive Italic scripts were generally developed in Italy and southern Europe, this particularly exuberant alphabet is the work of Dutch cartographer and mathematician Gerardus Mercator (1512–94), who in 1540 published a beautifully designed volume of writing samples. It offers a number of variations on the basic forms of the letters, demonstrating long ascenders and flourished tails, and also including the special features of the ampersands and ligatured letters. This is a finely written Italic with very little modulation in the letter strokes.

The controlled vigor of the flourishes ensures that they flow naturally from the lettering and do not interfere in any way with the legibility of the characters.

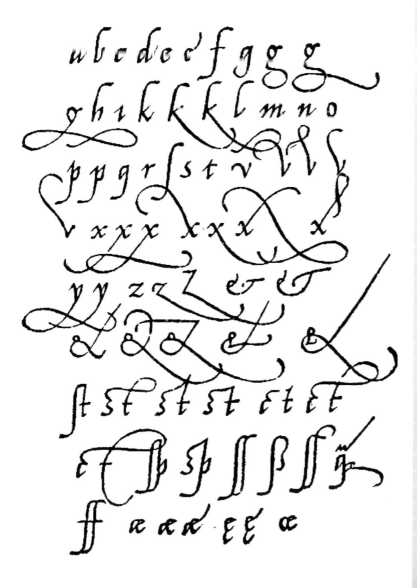

This Italic, produced by Gerardus Mercator, the leader of Dutch and Flemish cartographers, is restrained yet exuberant.

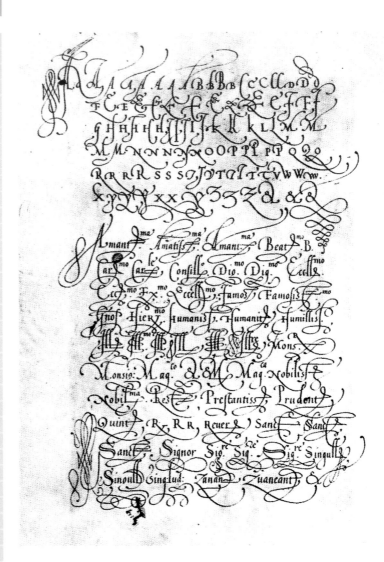

An incredibly rich example of Italic capital and lower-case letters. Although heavily flourished, it is an interesting source of inspiration.

ELABORATED ITALIC

The original manuscript, which prefaces a discourse on the art of hawking with Italic lettering samples, was written around 1560–70.

The light-textured capitals with their extended flourishes show the possible variety available in the basic letterforms. The final version of Z is a particularly curious and decorative construction. Here, the capitals are followed by a script sample containing further elaboration and finely drawn ornamentation.

As with earlier forms of lettering, Italic became widely used throughout Europe. During the main period of its prevalence, the style also developed differently in different countries and regions.

SPANISH ITALIC CAPITALS

Francisco Lucas (c. 1530 to after 1580) was an important influence on the development of Spanish calligraphy, perfecting his interpretations of the late Gothic cursive Bastarda, the Renaissance Humanistic scripts, and the rounded minuscules of Rotunda. This sample is a delightful exposition of variations in calligraphic form in an alphabet of capital letters: compact structures contrast with looped and flourished forms. The six different versions of M are particularly descriptive lessons in lettering design.

SPANISH ITALIC SCRIPT

This is a very fine and controlled Italic script, with a neat balance between the rising and descending lines and their relationships to the body height of the letters. The letterforms are well proportioned and evenly textured, the subtle slanting carried through in the tall curved ascenders and clubbed descenders. Distinctive variations of form include the forward and backward facing bowls of the g, the straight and curving versions of j, the abbreviated r, and the long and short forms of s. The alphabet is reproduced in woodcut, the letters being cut into the ground of the wood block rather than left raised upon the surface, thus printing as white on black.

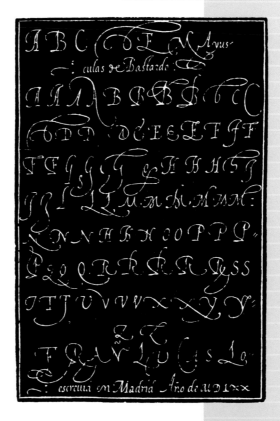

DECORATIVE ITALIC

This is a sixteenth-century copybook form, another sample in which the sharply elegant slanted Italic evolves under the influence of Copperplate engraving into a finely flourished, trailed, and ornamented style of capitals.

As was the usual practice in writing manuals, each letter is given in different versions. In this case, they vary from the oblique to the rounded, with decorative features from hooked or curving terminals to scrolled and woven ornamentation. The thick and thin variations of the letter strokes are not very pronounced. They suggest the original use of a pointed pen, with pressure applied to splay the nib slightly in order to broaden out the fine lines and soften the longer flourishes.

This engraved sample was published in England, but it shows the influence of Italian writing styles.

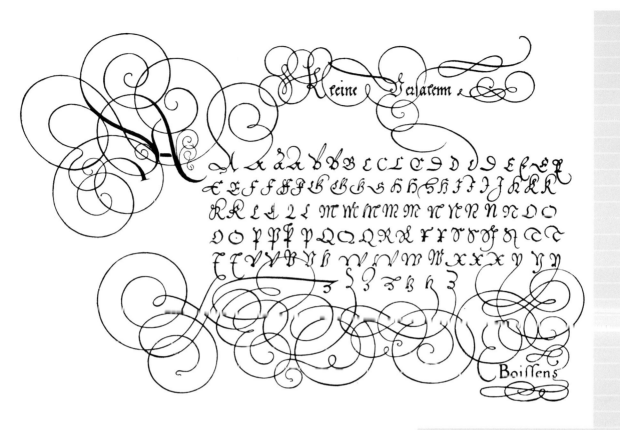

SLANTED GOTHIC

The characteristic slant of Italic is here applied to an elaborate style of lettering based on earlier Gothic forms. The sample is from a sixteenth-century Dutch copybook. The letterforms are inventively constructed, with full advantage taken of the fine pen line, which is twisted and looped into curious interpretations of each form.

In the more imaginative versions, notably B, G, P, and S, the character of the letter is taken so far beyond its recognizable shape and structure that seen out of context it would appear as a decorative abstract motif, calligraphic in influence but not necessarily identifiable as lettering.

In designing an alphabet sample it is acceptable to develop these ornamental qualities because the form is identified by its place in the letter sequence, though in a general text they might be less appropriate.

This design shows a keen appreciation of line, texture, and spatial balance, and demonstrates the graphic value and aesthetic pleasure of highly developed calligraphic skill.

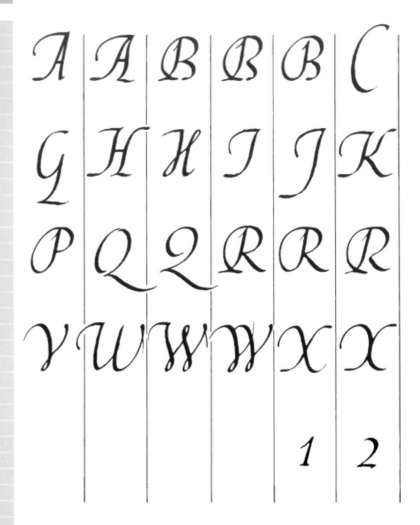

HUMANISTIC CURSIVE CAPITALS

Humanistic scripts were originally a southern European development based on the rounded ninth- and tenth-century minuscules. These upright and cursive hands were a product of the Renaissance period in Italy, in their turn giving rise to the compressed and angular Italic that is categorized as a Humanistic hand. The alternative forms in these cursive capitals reflect both the earlier influence and the development of the style. The slight slant is typical of Italic, as are the sharply turned angles of M and N, in this case incorporating fine, tight loops at the joining of the strokes in the head of each letter. But the letters also include a more fluid, rounded form of construction, still with an Italic-style branching of arch from the stem, but with a clearly

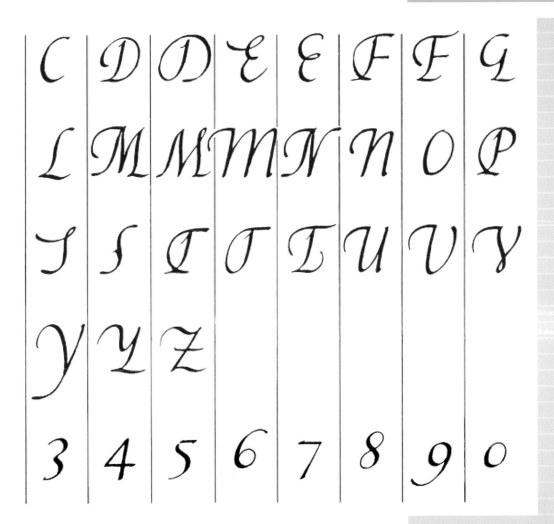

defined curve at the top of the
letters, and generous space
between terminals at the base.

The device of a leftward,
looping flourish from top to
bottom of a form helps to
balance the somewhat spidery,
tilted lettering.

Another modern interpretation
of a Humanistic majuscule
alphabet. The fluid, looped
forms in E and W suggest the
beginning of early Copperplate
characteristics.

Copperplate Alphabets

In the sixteenth century, the quality of rolled copper sheeting supplied to engravers improved dramatically. Lettering engravers were finally able to work with their burins on a surface comparable to the parchment used by scribes. Inspired by the newfound freedom expressed by the engravers, scribes abandoned their broad, square-cut quills for flexible, pointed nibs—and a fine, cursive writing emerged.

Copperplate could be rapidly written, dispensing with the need to lift the pen off the paper except for word and line breaks, and punctuation. The result was elegant lettering that flowed across the page. A pointed flexible nib responds well to pressure placed on it by the writer.

A major feature of Copperplate is the slight swelling of the downward strokes. This is acquired by applying a modicum of pressure to the pen as the stroke is made, thus forcing a little extra ink to flow through the now slightly separated point of the nib. Similarly, by releasing almost all the pressure on the upward stroke between the letters, an extraordinarily fine line is achieved.

Other readily identifiable characteristics of this hand are the occasional looped ascenders and descenders, and the graceful, flowing forms written at a slant of 54°. It is extremely awkward to write beautiful Copperplate without the correct equipment—either a pen with an elbow-angled nib, or an angled nib holder. The angle of the nib or holder provides the slant.

INCREASED LITERACY

The improvement in engraving techniques coincided with the increased levels of literacy that had developed after the advent of printing from movable type. People wanted to write and, in response to this interest, scribes prepared instructional copybooks. These were printed from metal plates, incised by engravers who executed exquisite, fine lines, flourished with an unlimited measure of ornamentation.

Copperplate lends itself to decoration—particularly energetic flourishing. If you look at old manuscripts written in any of the numerous cursive scripts, you will find grand pieces of penmanship rendered almost illegible. Here are beautifully executed letters disappearing in a subterfuge of ornament.

Copperplate became associated with more than handwritten lettering and printing. The lettering engravers exercised their art on items made of, for example, precious metal. Other craftspeople followed suit. Glass engravers, clockmakers, and metalsmiths acquired the elegant hand for their own purposes.

FORMING COPPERPLATE LETTERS

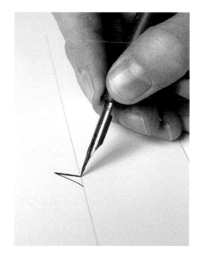 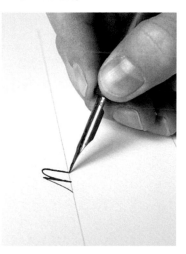 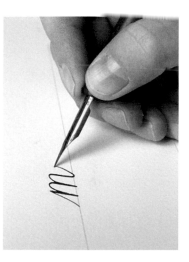

1 The letter shown here is being written with a fine straight nib. The letter begins with a hairline stroke, made with virtually no pressure on the nib so that it glides gracefully over the page. Gentle pressure is applied to the first vertical stroke, which finishes with a square end.

2 The second vertical stroke is preceded by another fine hairline stroke. Observe where the hairline leaves the first vertical stroke. Notice the shape of the white space formed by these two strokes.

3 Unlike the first two vertical strokes, which finished with a square end, the final stroke curves around into a hairline. This hairline is usually extended and becomes the first stroke of the next letter.

FOUR BASIC STROKES

This elegant script is composed of four basic strokes. The first is the hairline, which begins most of the letters. There is a further hairline, which serves as a ligature to join the letters. There are some strokes that have square ends. The final stroke to consider begins and ends with a hairline but swells in the middle as pressure is applied to force more ink through the nib.

The letters can be written with an elbow-angled holder or nib, or, with practice, a fine pointed nib. The slant of the writing is 45°, giving fine and flowing lines. The looped or flourished ascenders and descenders are generally of a greater length than those that finish straight.

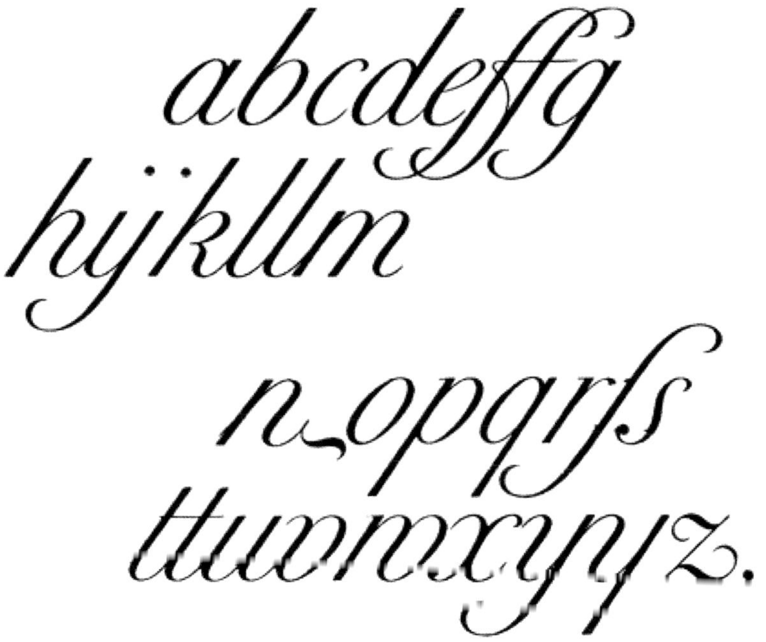

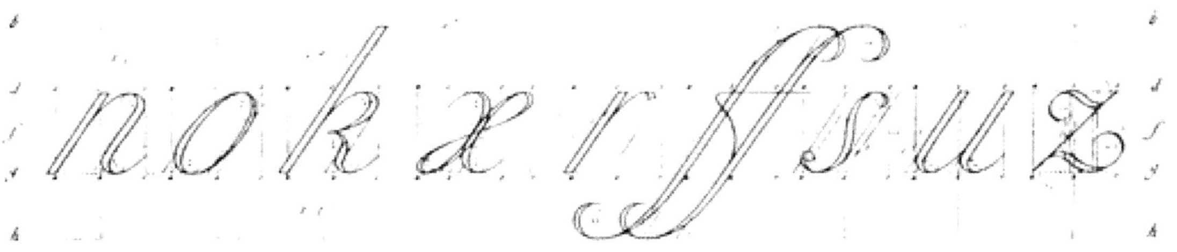

abcdeffg
hijkllm
nopqrfs
ttuvnxxyyz.

nokxrsſsuz

COPPERPLATE SCRIPT

This rather weighty Copperplate form, although rolling and cursive in style, is derived from an attempt to subject script lettering to a geometric system of construction. The letters are remarkably even and regular in proportion. The very straight and clean-cut ascenders and descenders are offered as an appropriate contrast to the elegantly curving tails. The relatively emphatic thick or thin modulation of the strokes refers back to the characteristic texture of edged pen writing.

However, in this case, it is artificially constructed by drawing with a pointed pen, outlining, and then filling the broader width of stems and curves, as may be seen in the samples of letter construction developed in a skeleton form within a carefully constructed grid format.

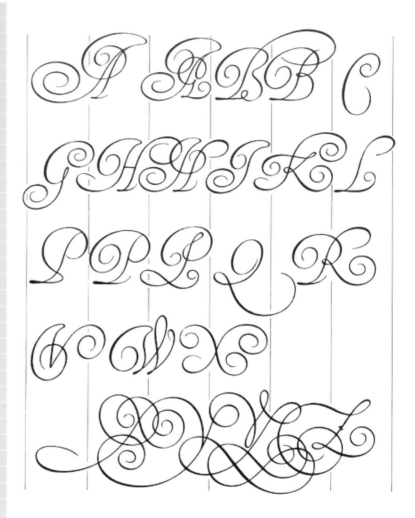

FLOURISHED CAPITALS

By the end of the sixteenth century, fine engraving on copper plates had superseded the broader printing technique of woodcut as a method of reproducing writing samples for publication. As the solid forms appropriate to woodcut had caused some modification to earlier pen lettering styles, so the fineness and fluidity of Copperplate engraving itself began to influence the fashion in writing styles, giving rise to the curling linear forms that became known as Copperplate scripts. The delicate swelling

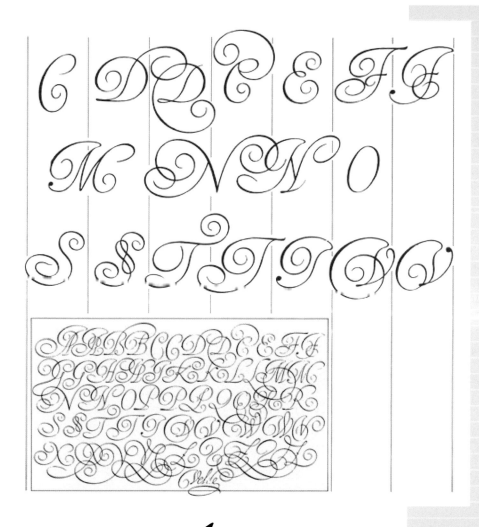

and narrowing line made by a graver corresponds to the traveling mark of a pointed pen guided under varying pressure. This impressive sample of Copperplate capitals has great movement, style, and energy, but it is controlled in the execution to produce harmoniously balanced relationships between the letters.

Jan Van den Velde, an accomplished Dutch calligrapher, designed this alphabet. The letters are beautifully conceived and expertly engraved.

FLOURISHED CAPITALS (1)

The proportions of these letters depart completely from the influence of standard traditional or classical forms.

The proliferation of styles that occurred with the widespread publication of copybooks led to much inventiveness in the design of letters, with greater and lesser degrees of success.

In the sample of looped capitals shown here there is a consistency in the relationships of the rounded letters, but A, H, M, N, and R are noticeably compressed, while X, Y, and Z are converted to comparatively broad forms.

Each letter appears to be developed in terms of its own structure, with less regard to the relationships between forms, especially in such details as the double curve of Q and the scrolled elaboration of X.

However, the key to the variations may lie in the fact that the alphabet, including all of the surrounding ornamentation, is conceived in terms of the overall design effect, and each grouping of letters has a definite internal coherence. These flourishes show the functional properties of the lettering.

These extremely finely engraved letters have unusual dot endings and elegant curves.

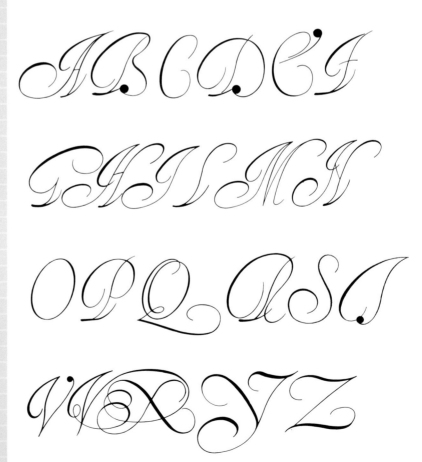

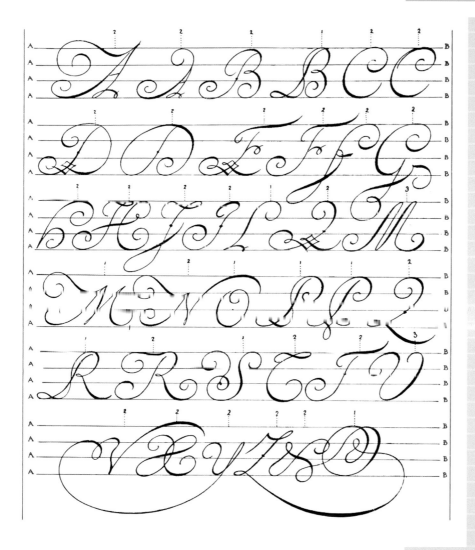

FLOURISHED CAPITALS (2)

These finely developed scrolled capitals demonstrate the versatility of Copperplate style. The thick/thin contrast betrays their origin as edged-pen rather than pointed pen letters, although the narrow nib width creates a fluid and lightweight appearance.

The construction of each letter is carefully controlled by the evenly spaced writing lines governing body height and internal features. The extended, looping flourishes at the heads and bases of the letters are systematically fitted to these guidelines.

The calligrapher, French writing master Charles Paillasson (fl. 1760), has allowed himself a final extravagant gesture in the billowing tails wrapped around the letters on the bottom line of the alphabet.

These free-flowing majuscule letters have the unusual additions of interlaced strapwork in D, E, and L.

POINTED PEN LETTERS (1)

This is an extremely refined, formal cursive script typical of the development of pointed pen lettering under the influence of Copperplate engraving in the eighteenth century. Its elegance derives from the compressed and elongated style. In the lower-case form, the length of ascenders and descenders exceeds the body height of the letters, but the evenness of the proportions maintains the overall balance of the script. The rounded capitals are elaborated with flowing, looped flourishes, while the subtly fluid stems of H, I, J, and K are topped with an intriguing double curve.

The numerals, although consistent with the overall style of the lettering, are a little more generous in width, but they are carefully contained within a fixed body height.

This alphabet combines round and pointed capitals.

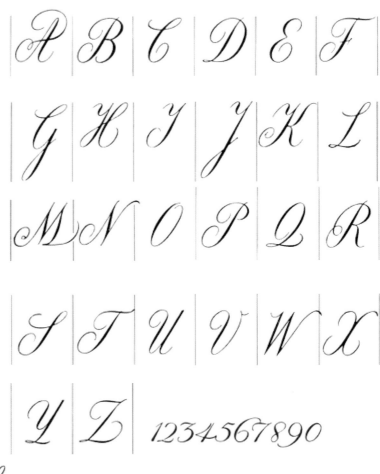

POINTED PEN LETTERS (2)

The lightweight, flowing texture of pointed pen writing has a gracefulness seen at its best when an alphabet form is designed, like this sample, as a series of well-proportioned, unelaborated shapes.

The loops and curls are restrained and naturally in harmony with the basic structure of each letter. The cursive nature of the script is demonstrated in the finely slanted joining strokes forming discreet links between the letters.

The relationships between the script, capitals, and numerals are completely consistent and appropriate, including the alternative rounded and angular forms shown for the capital letters M, N, V, and W.

This alphabet shows some alternative letters, for example, M and N.

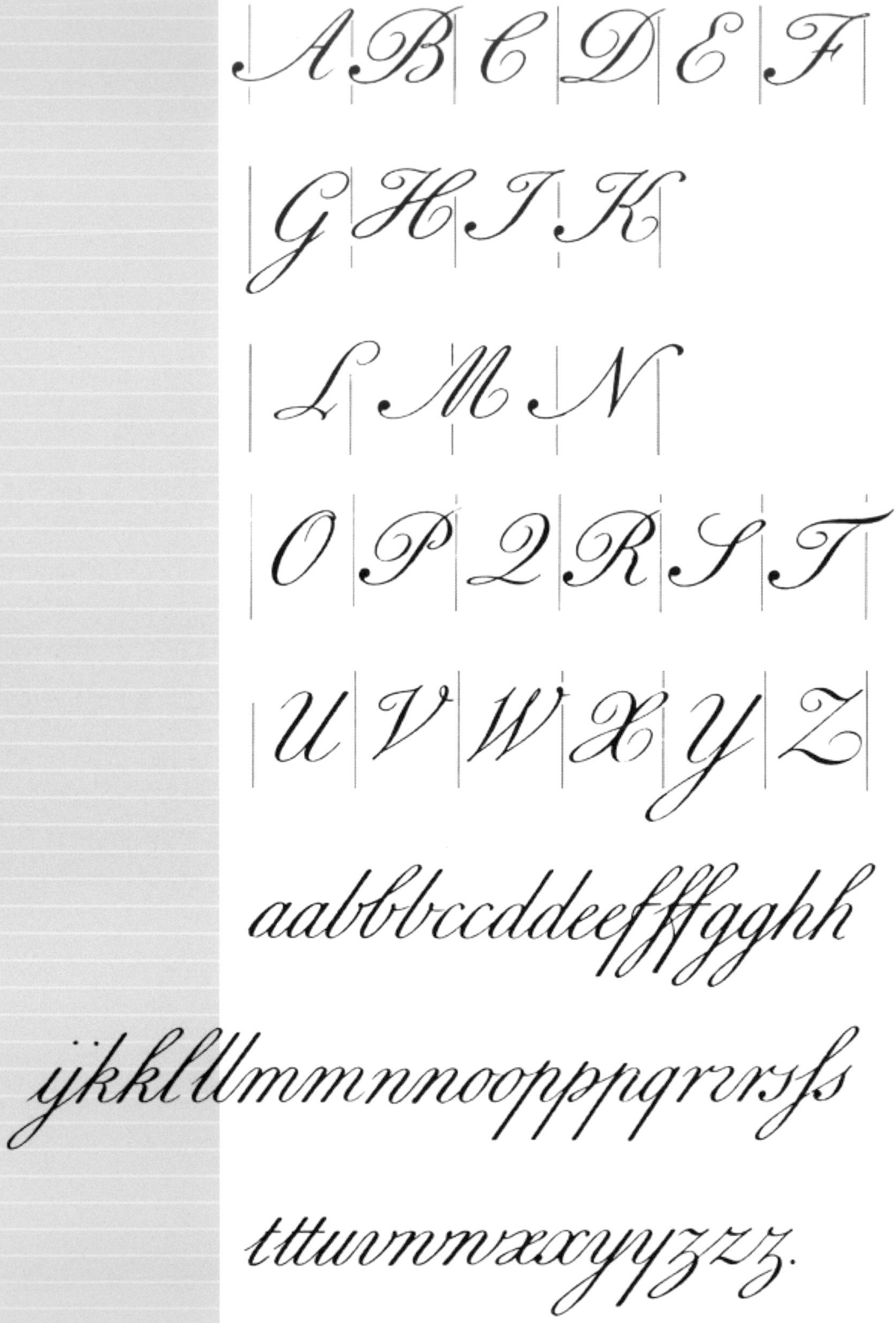

A B C D E F

G H I J K

L M N

O P Q R S T

U V W X Y Z

aabbccddeefffgghh

ijkkllllmmmnnnooppppqrrrrsʃs

tttuvvnnxxxyyzzz.

Aabbcdefffghhbiijjkkkllmn ohpqgrzsfstttuvvnxxyyyz

ROUNDHAND

English Copperplate script of the eighteenth century demonstrates a refined and even hand in which the smoothly curving letterforms are slanted and cursive. This is a prime example of lettering designed specifically to be reproduced by engraving. The pointed pen moves fluidly through the form of each letter, and the varying pressure used to modulate the pen line has been subtly applied and carefully controlled. This is a decorative but not elaborate script, the lower-case letters being finely balanced and embellished with loops, while the capitals are evenly matched and developed with elegantly restrained flourishes. The engraving, though not the original lettering, was carried out by the English calligrapher and master engraver George Bickham (c. 1684–1748). His collection of writing samples was published serially under the title *The Universal Penman*, and was highly influential on contemporary writing style.

ROUND TEXT

The round hand is, like the earlier forms of Italic writing, an elegant but extremely practical hand, well adapted to the natural movement of hand and pen.

This cursive sample shows the linking of letters through the flowing motion of the pen along the writing line, facilitated by the slanting of the letters. The body height of the letters is equal to the length of the ascenders, and a subtle balance is created by the extended drop of the descenders looping below the baseline.

The forms are compressed, but the rounded bowls and arches maintain the even texture of the script in the relationship between height and width of the letters. This evenness is also due to the consistency of the pen strokes, in which the minimal variation of pressure and density is fluidly applied.

FINE GOTHIC-STYLE SCRIPT

The fashion for copybooks in the eighteenth century encouraged the most versatile displays of calligraphic skill, and the technique of Copperplate engraving was not employed solely to reproduce the style of current pointed pen lettering. Whereas the Gothic-influenced script, which the original publication terms "German text," refers to the earlier style of edged-pen letters, the tools of engraving require that a heavy black line be built up from several finely cut lines. This sample shows a modification to the letterforms with regard to the influence of that technique. The lower-case letters are made light in texture and slightly flourished. The tails and ascenders, though complementary, do not extend naturally from the angular, pointed structures but seem to be an addition based on contemporary fashion. The capitals are more heavily defined but decorated with finely looped ornamentation. This balance of texture ensures that the letters emerge as distinct and legible despite the elaboration.

SQUARE TEXT

Square text is the name given in the original copybook publication to this eighteenth-century calligraphy based on Gothic forms. It is an appropriate designation: although the letters are angularized by the pointed terminals and lozenge-shaped serifs borrowed from Blackletter styles, these are grafted onto an adaptation of rounded letters that gives the script a broad, squared quality and medium-weight texture identifiably of its own period, though influenced by the historical source. In the capital letters, the extended, looping hairlines enhance the lively character of the text. Certain authentic medieval letterforms show this type of hairline embellishment, but in this case again, the manner of execution seems

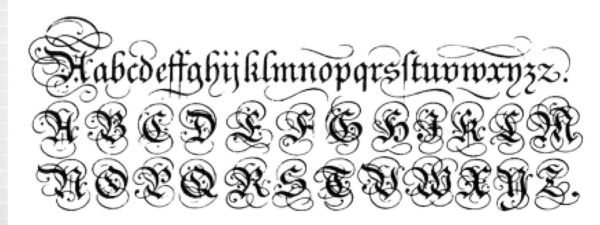

A B C D E F G H I J K L M,
a b c d e f f g h i j k l m n o p q r s s t u v w x y z
N O P Q R S T V V W X Y Z

to owe more to contemporary fashion than to the origin of the device. But the overall structure of the capital letters and the divided counters of C, G, O, Q, and T possess a convincing period flavor.

REVISED HUMANISTIC SCRIPTS

These two samples draw upon the characteristics of Renaissance hands to develop script letters of sharp angularity matched by more generous, flowing capitals. The first is an inventive, eclectic script; the pairing of capital and small letters suggests that it is developed within its own terms of reference rather than strictly based on a known traditional style. The cursive script originally designated the "secretary" hand, which forms the second sample, is a very tightly constructed, logical, and balanced form which, as the name suggests, was intended to be highly functional in day-to-day tasks requiring writing that was rapid but refined, consistent, and legible.

Aa Bb Cc Dd Ee Ff Gg Hh Ii Jj Kk Ll Mm Nn Oo
Pp Qq Rr Ss Tt Uu Vv Ww Xx Yy Zz

Aa mb cc nd me nf ng nh ni nj nk nl nn nm ny np nr ns nt nu nv nw nx ny nz
A B C D E F G H I J K L M N O P Q R S T V W X Y Z

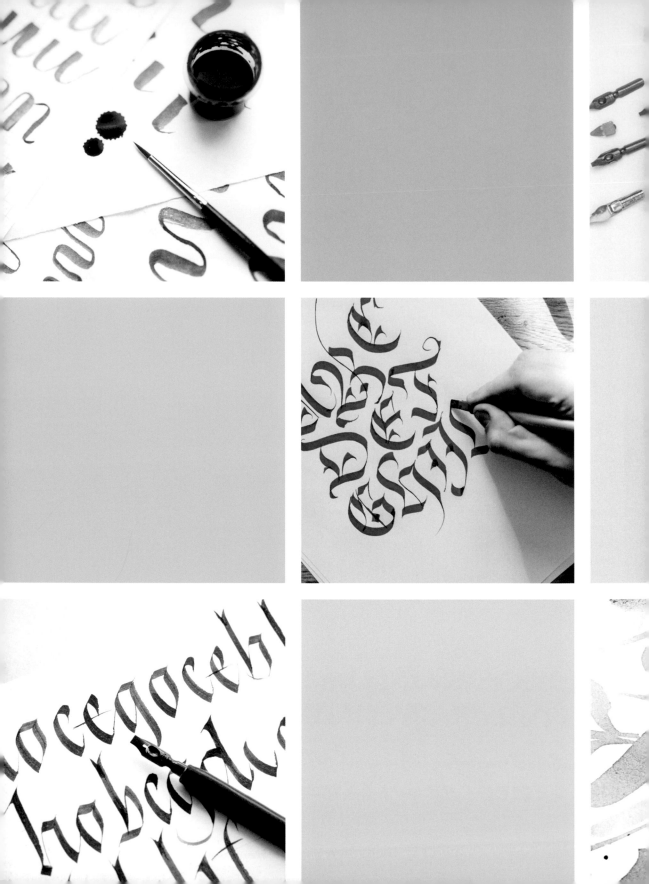

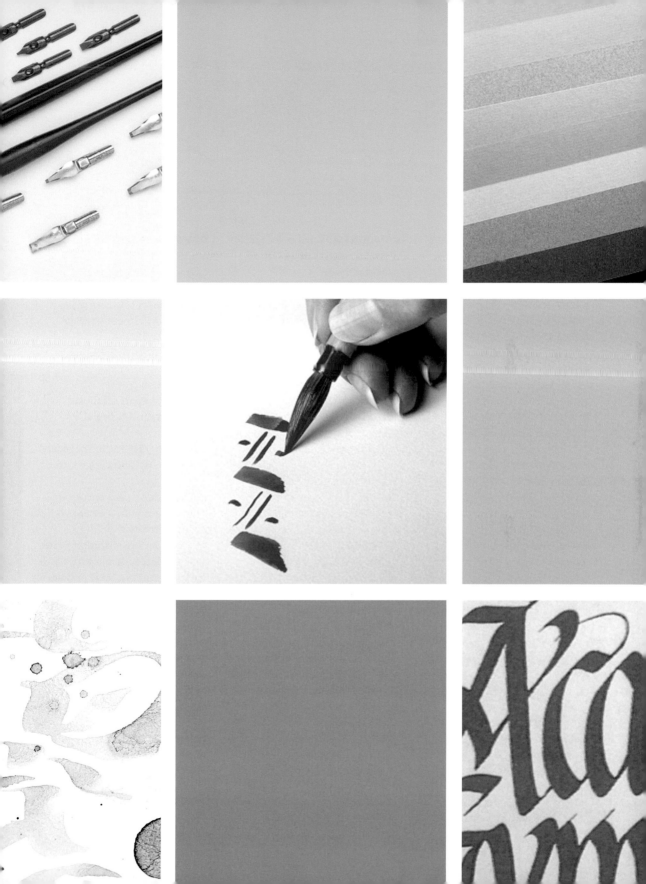

Glossary

ARCH The part of a LOWER-CASE letter formed by a curve springing from the STEM of the letter, as in h, m, n.

ASCENDER The rising stroke of a LOWER-CASE letter.

BASELINE Also called the writing line, this is the level on which a line of writing rests, giving a fixed reference for the relative heights of letters and the drop of DESCENDERS.

BLACKLETTER The term for the dense, angular writing of the GOTHIC period.

BODY HEIGHT The height of the basic form of a LOWER-CASE letter, not including the extra length of ASCENDERS or DESCENDERS.

BOOK HAND Any style of alphabet commonly used in book production before the age of printing.

BOUSTROPHEDON An arrangement of lines of writing, used by the Greeks, in which alternate lines run in opposite directions.

BOWL The part of a letter formed by curved strokes attaching to the main STEM and enclosing a COUNTER, as in R, P, a, b.

BROADSHEET A design in calligraphy contained on a single sheet of paper, vellum, or parchment.

BUILT-UP LETTERS Letters formed by drawing rather than writing, or having modifications to the basic form of the structural pen strokes.

CALLIGRAM Words or lines of writing arranged to construct a picture or design.

CAROLINGIAN SCRIPT The first standard MINUSCULE script, devised by Alcuin of York under the direction of Emperor Charlemagne at the end of the eighth century.

CHANCERY CURSIVE A form of ITALIC script used by the scribes of the papal Chancery in Renaissance Italy, also known as cancellaresca.

CHARACTER A typographic term to describe any letter, punctuation mark, or symbol commonly used in typesetting.

CODEX A book made up of folded and/or bound leaves forming successive pages.

COLOPHON An inscription at the end of a handwritten book giving details of the date, place, scribe's name, or other such relevant information.

COUNTER The space within a letter wholly or partially enclosed by the lines of the letterform, within the BOWL of P, for example.

CROSS-STROKE A horizontal stroke essential to the SKELETON form of a letter, as in E, F, T.

CUNEIFORM The earliest systematic form of writing, taking its name from the wedge-shaped strokes made when inscribing on soft clay.

CURSIVE A handwriting form where letters are fluidly formed and joined, without pen lifts.

DEMOTIC SCRIPT The informal SCRIPT of the Egyptians, following on from HIEROGLYPHS and HIERATIC SCRIPT.

DESCENDER The tail of a LOWER-CASE letter that drops below the BASELINE.

DIACRITICAL SIGN An accent or mark that indicates particular pronunciation.

DUCTUS The order of strokes followed in constructing a pen letter.

FACE (abb. TYPEFACE) The general term for an alphabet designed for typographic use.

FLOURISH An extended pen stroke or linear decoration used to embellish a basic letterform.

GESSO A smooth mixture of plaster and white lead bound in gum, which can be reduced to a liquid medium for writing or painting.

GILDING Applying gold leaf to an adhesive base to decorate a letter or ORNAMENT.

GOTHIC SCRIPT A broad term embracing a number of different styles of writing, characteristically angular and heavy, of the late medieval period.

HAIRLINE The finest stroke of a pen, often used to create SERIFS and other finishing strokes, or decoration of a basic letterform.

HAND An alternative term for handwriting or SCRIPT, meaning lettering written by hand.

HIERATIC SCRIPT The formal SCRIPT of the Ancient Egyptians.

HIEROGLYPHS The earliest form of writing used by the Ancient Egyptians, in which words were represented by pictorial symbols.

IDEOGRAM A written symbol representing a concept or abstract idea rather than an actual object.

ILLUMINATION The decoration of a MANUSCRIPT with gold leaf burnished to a high shine; the term is also used more broadly to describe decoration in gold and colors.

INDENT To leave space additional to the usual margin when beginning a line of writing, as in the opening of a paragraph.

IONIC SCRIPT The standard form of writing developed by the Greeks.

ITALIC Slanted forms of writing with curving letters based on an elliptical rather than circular model.

LAYOUT The basic plan of a two-dimensional design, showing spacing, organization of text, illustration, and so on.

LOGO A word or combination of letters designed as a single unit, sometimes combined with a decorative or illustrative element; it may be used as a trademark, emblem, or symbol.

LOWER CASE Typographic term for "small" letters, as distinct from capitals, which are known in typography as upper case.

MAJUSCULE A capital letter.

MANUSCRIPT A term used specifically for a book or document written by hand rather than printed.

MASSED TEXT Text written in a heavy or compressed SCRIPT and with narrow spacing between words and lines.

MINUSCULE A "small" or LOWER-CASE letter.

ORNAMENT A device or pattern used to decorate handwritten or printed text.

PALAEOGRAPHY The study of written forms, including the general development of alphabets and particulars of handwritten manuscripts, such as date, provenance, and so on.

PALIMPSEST A manuscript from which a text has been erased and the writing surface used again.

PAPYRUS The earliest form of paper, a coarse material made by hammering together strips of fiber from the stem of the papyrus plant.

PARCHMENT Writing material prepared from the inner layer of a split sheepskin.

PHONOGRAM A written symbol representing a sound in speech.

PICTOGRAM A pictorial symbol representing a particular object or image.

RAGGED TEXT A page or column of writing with lines of different lengths, which are aligned at neither side.

RIVER The appearance of a vertical rift in a page of text, caused by an accidental, but consistent, alignment of word spaces on following lines.

ROMAN CAPITALS The formal alphabet of capital letters devised by the Romans, which was the basis of most modern, western alphabet systems.

RUBRICATE To contrast or emphasize part or parts of a text by writing in red; for example headings, a prologue, a quotation.

RUSTIC CAPITALS An informal alphabet of capital letters used by the Romans, with letters elongated and rounded compared to the standard square ROMAN CAPITALS.

SANS SERIF A term denoting letters without SERIFS or finishing strokes.

SCRIPT Another term for writing by hand, often used to imply a CURSIVE style of writing.

SCRIPTORIUM A writing room, particularly that of a medieval monastery in which formal manuscripts were produced.

SERIF An abbreviated pen stroke or device used to finish the main stroke of a letterform; a HAIRLINE or hook, for example.

SKELETON LETTER The most basic form of a letter, demonstrating its essential distinguishing characteristics.

STEM The main vertical stroke in a letterform.

TEXTURA A term for particular forms of GOTHIC SCRIPT that were so dense and regular as to appear to have a woven texture. Textura is a Latin word, meaning "weave."

TRANSITIONAL SCRIPT A letterform marking a change in style between one standard SCRIPT and the development of a new form.

UNCIAL A book hand used by the Romans and early Christians, typified by the heavy, squat form of the rounded O.

VELLUM Writing material prepared from the skin of a calf, having a particularly smooth, velvety texture.

VERSAL A large, decorative letter used to mark the opening of a line, paragraph, or verse in a MANUSCRIPT.

WEIGHT A measurement of the relative size and thickness of a pen letter, expressed by the relationship of nib width to height.

WORD BREAK The device of hyphenating a word between syllables so it can be split into two sections to regulate line length in a text. Both parts, ideally, should be pronounceable.

X-HEIGHT Typographic term for BODY HEIGHT.

Index